Living with Snakes and other Reptiles

dedicated to

Elle-Angelique Watharow

SIMON WATHAROW

Living with Snakes and other Reptiles

PUBLISHING

National Library of Australia Cataloguing-in-Publication entry

Watharow, Simon, 1967–
Living with snakes and other reptiles / by Simon Watharow.

9780643097216 (pbk.)
9780643097223 (epdf)
9780643103818 (epub)

Includes bibliographical references and index.
Snakes – Australia.
Snakes – Behavior – Australia.
Reptiles – Australia.
Reptiles – Behavior – Australia.

597.90994

Published by
CSIRO PUBLISHING
36 Gardiner Road, Clayton VIC 3168
Private Bag 10, Clayton South VIC 3169
Australia

Telephone: [+613] 9545 8555
Local call: 1300 788 000 (Australia only)
Fax: +61 3 9662 7555
Email: csiropublishing@csiro.au
Web site: www.publishing.csiro.au

Set in Myriad Pro 9/13
Cover design: Andrew Weatherill
Layout and design: Oryx Publishing
Printed by Ingram Lightning Source

Feb26_RP_ILS

Contents

Green Python. Image: Lyall Naylor

Acknowledgements

Eastern Brown Snake.

Thanks to the Watharow family: Patrick, Myra, Annmaree, Sean, Damian and Fleur who have all contributed significantly through their support, encouragement and help. Angela Reid supported and sacrificed beyond the duties of a partner.

Heartfelt thanks to the following photographers for generous use of their images: Martin Baxter, Brian Bush, John Cann, Nick Clemann, CSL Ltd, Rebecca Cockburn, Steven Cook, Simon Fearn, Greg Fyfe, Ken Griffith, Michael Lentic, Byron Manning, Brad Maryan, Stewart McDonald, Peter Mirtschin, Lyall Naylor, Ian Norton, Paul Orange, Jon Simmons and John Weigel.

The following provided assistance with animals, field trips and photography: Michael Alexander, Martin Baxter, Darron Cameron, Terry Cook, Lyall Naylor, Sharon Small and the Australian Reptile Park. My special thanks go to Steven Cook for his significant help.

My thanks are due to a number of people for help and text additions. Charlie Manolis reviewed the crocodile section, while Peter Mirtchin, Lyall Naylor, Brian Bush, Ken Griffiths and Chris Pederby reviewed some of the snake species accounts and helped with catcher call-outs, for their respective states. Dr Jay Harley kindly provided the cartoons and Chris Pederby assisted with data and images from the Northern Territory. The Kimberley Toadbusters and Graeme Sawyer provided assistance with the section on the Cane Toad.

Thanks also to Ruth Duncan, Dr Adam Skinner, Maria Kouveli and Keiran Ragas from CSL Ltd.

My gratitude to Nick Alexander for all his patience and help with this book, and special thanks to all those snakes that never bit me!

Simon Watharow
simon@snakeline.com.au

1 Introduction

Australia is home to a diverse and amazing range of reptiles – we have more than 1000 species that live in many different habitats across the continent. Most reptiles are adapted to live in a specific habitat, and some of these habitats can be quite threatened by environmental disturbances such as erosion, logging, salinity, introduced vegetation or animals, removal of rocks, and, of course, urban development. In a few cases reptiles have adapted to exist – but rarely thrive – in urban environments and it is here that contact between people and reptiles is more frequent.

Over the last 200 years, Australians have built up a very strong negative image of reptiles, especially snakes, and this negative image has been reinforced by many fallacies and misconceptions. This book, therefore, aims to shed new light on these creatures and provide the reader with

The Oenpelli Rock Python occurs in the rocky escarpments of Arnhem Land, Northern Territory. Image: John Weigel

As its name suggests, the Water Python is often associated with bodies of water. Image: John Weigel

A Lowland Copperhead basking in the sun. Image: John Weigel

the knowledge to better cope with reptiles in backyards, the workplace and in their natural habitats.

At one time or another, most Australians have had contact with a snake. Stories abound of near death experiences with a hissing snake that stares into the person's eyes, or makes a mock strike or an attack. Often the size of the snake is exaggerated into an anaconda serpent that can leap buildings!

In most encounters the threat from a snake is minimal and people need basic, common sense to manage the situation. A snake views a human as a predator yet, strangely, we imagine the snake to have a predatory role as an attacker. Fear can inadvertently be the cause of a bite because the person, concerned for their family, makes an attempt to kill the snake thus increasing their chance of being bitten.

In all my time dealing with reptiles, I have never heard of a snake, left alone, that has bitten a person. Most snakebite occurs during confrontations, when people engage in risky behaviour such as trying to catch them or poking them, or when backyards are so snake friendly that they encourage frequent visits. There are certainly some cases of misadventure when a snake is accidentally trodden on.

Some 3000–4000 snakebites occur each year in Australia. Most of these are bites from harmless snakes or bites where snake venom was not injected, often because the person's clothing has defeated the bite. Of all these snake bites only around 200–300 will become envenomed and there may be one or two deaths during the year. Not bad odds!

Serious snakebite usually happens when someone deliberately interferes with a snake or when they try to harm it. Snakes need to be left alone. They tend to have a beneficial impact on the environment, often helping to control pest species such as mice or starlings that are found around our properties.

Most snakes have a nervous disposition and are quick to hide or flee when approached. Others rely heavily on

Most bites from a Desert Death Adder occur when a person accidentally steps on a well camouflaged and immobile snake. Image: Greg Fyfe.

camouflage to go unnoticed. Some have strong defence displays which are intended to send you, the predator, a strong message – keep away!

Snakes and other reptiles need our protection, their habitats conserved and their biodiversity maintained for future generations. The misguided saying, 'The only good snake is a dead snake', needs to be removed from our vocabulary.

Although they present a small risk, lizards, too, can frighten people. All Australian lizards are relatively harmless, although some of the larger monitor lizards are capable of inflicting a serious wound. Some lizards have been successful in surviving in urban regions. Blue-tongue lizards, for example, tend to become established in suburban gardens where snails are abundant.

In northern Australia, crocodiles can cause concern. These feared predators are a wonderful and exciting prehistoric relic – dinosaurs still alive today! It amazes

The Eastern Blue-tongue Lizard is the most common lizard seen in yards across eastern to northern Australia. In the southern states its banding may frighten some people due to the similarity to the dangerously venomous Eastern Tiger Snake, which often occurs in the same habitats as blue-tongue lizards.

A Saltwater Crocodile displays its awesome teeth while basking.

The dreaded invading Cane Toad is a common sight in backyards of northern Australia.

me that we can, on the one hand, fuss over historic buildings only a few hundred years old, yet ruthlessly kill off an incredible living fossil that has managed to survive millions of years of evolutionary development. Little is known about these long-lived reptiles. Ironically most of what we know comes from the fact we farm them for food and fashion items.

Cane Toads now have a place in our landscape, too, having taken up permanent residency in Australia. The abundance of waterways in northern and eastern Australia sustains their growing spread. These animals have had a major impact on many native species and have become a nuisance in urban environments where outside lights attract their main prey – invertebrates. This book includes a short section for those faced with the task of living with Cane Toads.

Each year there are more than 15 000 calls for help in relation to a snake around someone's home or property, and a large percentage of these require a specialist snake catcher to attend. Often the snake catcher finds a snake-friendly yard which, ironically, usually remains unchanged even after his advice has been given and the snake has

The Eastern Brown Snake has adapted to human-made changes better than any other snake. It is now a common problem snake in most states except Tasmania and is responsible for most snake bites and the occasional death.

been removed. This book looks at the various means of snake prevention and tools to help minimise snakes around the house.

Each capital city has a specific range of species that are commonly encountered in backyards (see Appendix, page 134). Brown snakes certainly are the most abundant snakes in rural and major cities (except Tasmania) and are the most likely cause of snakebite and, possibly, death. There is a strong tendency for there to be more harmless snakes the further north you go. Melbourne, Hobart, Perth and Adelaide metropolitan regions predominantly have only dangerously venomous snakes, while Brisbane, Darwin and Sydney (to a lesser extent) have a larger complement of harmless snakes.

The way we present our gardens, with large ponds, rodent infestations and nestling birds in the roof eaves usually is the 'welcome mat' for passing snakes. 'Have I come to Eden!' says the snake.

I hope this book will shed some light on ways best to reduce snake attracting gardens and yards. Like fire prevention techniques, snake prevention techniques will help reduce the threat considerably.

2 Snakes in history

Throughout human history our cultural beliefs and folklore have formed the basis for much of our understanding of snakes. Nearly all cultures in the world have snake legends. Many have worshipped serpents and in some cultures they are revered. The ability of snakes to shed their skin has, in folklore and legend, given them the supernatural ability to rejuvenate the spirit – or life itself. Palaeolithic people often had markings of snakes on their weapons. Religion, too, has played a significant role in shaping our attitude towards them. Perhaps the most famous Western belief is the snake in the Garden of Eden, and its trickery of Adam and Eve into original sin.

Throughout human history the snake has played a sinister role. Adam and Eve being tempted by the serpent in a 1504 woodcut by Alfred Dürer.

The Indian Cobra is a leading cause of snakebite in Asian and the sub-continent countries. It is also heavily featured in the folklore and legends within these cultures. Its famous hooded stance is recognised worldwide. Image: Peter Mirtschin

The snake is quite different from a mammal. For some it represents the 'other side of humanity' or the darker mysterious forces in nature. These frightening associations are sometimes represented physically in the form of a snake. Snakes also have the ability to suddenly appear and as quickly disappear; this – combined with the ability of venomous snakes to kill – has lent the snake an aura of godlike qualities.

The famous Hopi Rain Dance, which is still part of the culture of Mexican people in Arizona, is used to send messages to their rain gods. It involves dancing with live snakes.

In Buddhism, the snake appears in the 'Wheel of Birth and Death' – the incessant cycle of existence in which all beings are trapped. The centre of the wheel contains a rooster, a snake and a pig, representing the root causes that keep us trapped in this cycle. The rooster represents greed, the snake, aversion, and the pig, delusion or ignorance. 'Nagas' are a compilation of snake-like beings that perform a range of deeds, both favourable (when

In Hindu and Buddhist religions, 'Nagas' are traditionally used to represent snakes, both for protection and as a sign of reverence.

revered) and destructive (when angered). It is said that, during the Buddha's enlightenment, a naga protected him from the destructive weather elements for seven days by covering him in the guise of a cobra hood.

Australian Aboriginal paintings of the 'Rainbow Serpent' are believed to have been done about 6000 years ago. The Rainbow Serpent is depicted as a long mythical creature made of the parts of different animals – the head of a kangaroo or a flying fox, and the tail of a crocodile, joined by the body of a huge water python decorated with water lilies, yams and waving tendrils. The Rainbow Serpent is most likely a symbolic representation of the Water Python, *Liasis fuscus,* that mysteriously disappears during the dry season but suddenly reappears in large numbers when the wet season arrives. The serpent was believed to be a creator of people, with life-giving powers that send conception spirits to all the waterholes. It was the personification of fertility, regenerating rains and increase in good seasons, and also of storms and floods which were a sign of transgressions.

Buddha meditates while a naga spreads its hood above him to protect him from the rain.

The mysterious Water Python most likely provides the inspiration for the legend of the Rainbow Serpent. Image: Lyall Naylor

A day's slaughter on the Murray River in 1906.

Source: National Library of Austrralia.

In earlier times, snakes and their bites have been treated by various bizarre, dangerous and ineffective methods. Often it was a case of 'an eye for an eye' – some treatments included ingesting the snake's head, or biting its body! A Hindu belief was to bite the head of the offending snake and render its venom harmless. Old and New World cultures sometimes used snake faeces to treat wounds with patients being buried up to their necks as part of the supposed cure. Nineteenth and early twentieth century treatments included sucking wounds or plugging them with small stones ('snakestones') in order to remove the venom or other diseases.

Later on ligature followed by amputation of the bitten limb was an unfortunate method of treatment by doctors in Western cultures. Alcohol was used in American and Australian early days – it was assumed that giving brandy or whisky would somehow change the course of snakebite.

'Old timers' in the Australian snake shows all had their own treatments for snakebite including burning 'Condy's

One of Australia's most serious and impressive threat displays – an Eastern Brown Snake rearing to its full height, mouth open and about to strike. Image: Ken Griffiths

crystals', a preparation of potassium permanganate. Some of them had a self-proclaimed immunity to snakebite – a belief that often led to fatal consequences.

* * *

Myths and misconceptions still abound. Australia is sometimes claimed to have the 'world's deadliest' snakes. However, 'deadly' means more than just venom toxicity, we also need to take into account the amount of venom the snake may inject and the depth of the injection. In Australia, the risk of a fatal bite is low, especially compared to the risk in countries with just as venomous snakes and poor access to medical treatment. Worldwide estimates of death by snakebite vary from 60 000–125 000, with India, Sri Lanka and Bangladesh being among the major snakebite regions. In countries such as these, a trip to work in the rice paddy may result in death, with no recourse to help.

A late 19th century kit for the treatment of snakebite included chloride of lime. Image courtesy John Cann.

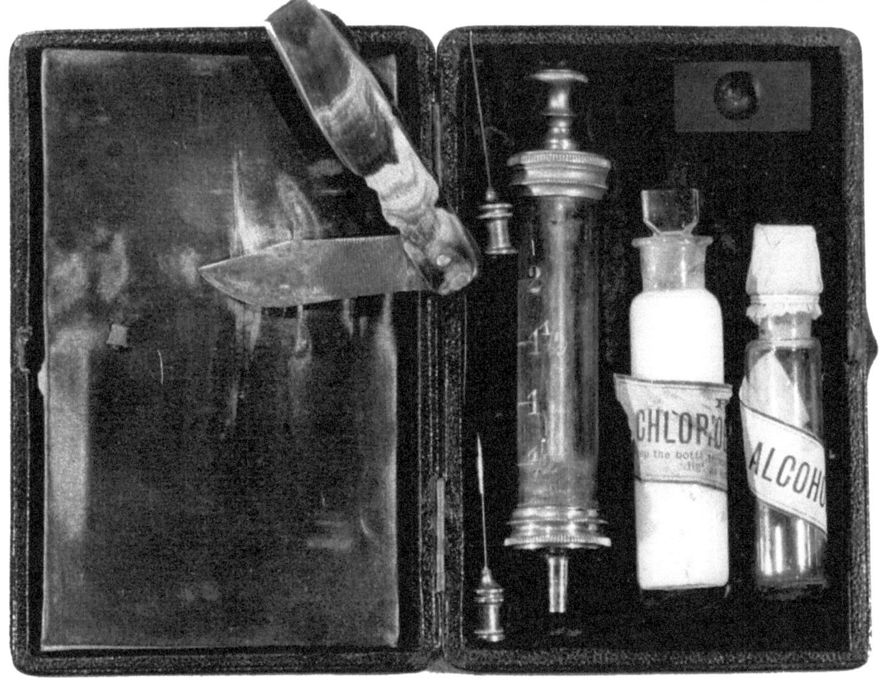

A Southern Death Adder can often be found in among washed-up seaweed on the shore.

Image: John Weigel

Australia, by contrast, has a well-equipped range of medical services to deal with snakebite. The ability to phone the Royal Flying Doctors Service from anywhere in the country, plus major call centres and advisory lines all set Australia apart in the worldwide snakebite arena. The major producer of antivenom – CSL Ltd – supplies hospitals and veterinarian practices. All Australian snakes are covered by specific and non-specific antivenoms. We also have a good network of services for 'nuisance' reptiles from wildlife rescue groups to commercial operators for snakes.

3 Why do we fear snakes?

Fear of snakes – ophidiophobia – is one of the most common fears throughout the world. Over the years, it has led to a variety of fables and fallacies. What makes people afraid of snakes? When confronted by a snake, people react differently, but familiar signs may include faintness, palpitations, sweating, nervousness or anxiety.

Fear is a strong survival instinct and, as part of our instinct for self-preservation, it allows us to train for conflict in our world. Evolution is selective, that is people who are naturally fearful manage to survive and pass their respective survival traits along. So why would a fearful person put their life in jeopardy by taking on a dangerous snake? It seems that what we fear most will happen because we behave in a manner that will cause it!

This man had never handled a snake till I gave him a 4 m Scrub Python called 'Kairn' to hold. The snake is perfectly happy being handled by people. Would you be happy to handle it?

Q These four snakes may be found along a waterway in Queensland. Which ones are harmless?

A All of them! But it had you guessing! It's best to treat all snakes as venomous – even trained herpetologists are not always sure. Clockwise from top left, the species are: Water Python, Keelback, Slaty-grey Snake, and Macleay's Water Snake.

Image: Lyall Naylor

From my observations, it certainly appears that people of Anglo-Saxon background seem to be more fearful of snakes. Perhaps it is because they have evolved in countries with little or no contact with snakes. People from Asia, South America or Africa seem to take the threat of snakes more in their stride. Perhaps a greater exposure to a wide range of serious animal threats has trained them to handle their anxiety more effectively?

A refreshingly different sign in Western Australia warning people that tiger snakes are protected.

Fears may also be the result of a bad experience or hearing a 'horror snake story' told when a person is very young, which leaves a strong negative emotion. It is often a result of misinformation that people are scared of snakes at all. It hardly seems logical that these simple, basic animals make some people afraid. Fear is a complex and relatively uncontrollable beast that some people have roaming around in their thoughts.

During my years as a snake-catcher, I often heard terror in voices over the telephone, and arrived expecting to see a gigantic 2 m striking serpent, only to find a small terrified 40 cm tiger snake trying to hide. Interestingly enough, people would then surround me and ask a dozen questions and suddenly see this small snake in a different light. They would notice the attractive colours and then say 'It's kind of pretty' and 'It's a lot smaller than I remember'! Fear seems to exaggerate our perceptions, and once the snake is in the bag, the rational side of the brain takes over again. If I have been called again by the same people, on a second occasion, the call is usually more calm and measured. The snake is described more accurately – perhaps 'It's lazing in the sun' and 'When you are free, can you come and get it?'. The fear of the unknown has been overcome.

To conquer your fear you need to be armed with the facts so that you can manage your fear effectively. Often facing your fear is the very best step you can take. If you learn about what scares you, you are then able to confront it and say 'I will not be scared any more'.

Reptile demonstrations have done a lot to reveal the true nature of reptiles and change longstanding incorrect beliefs.
Image: Ken Griffiths

Facing your fears is a very important tool to use in everyday life.

It is common for people who handle and display snakes to see the fear in some audience members. Some people's fear revolves around the way a snake looks, its fixed gaze, its strong coils and menacing posture, or the way it glides around. Others are terrified of being bitten. It is inspiring to watch a person face their fear for the first time and actually touch a snake, then change from having rigid, sweating and jerky movements into being gentle and more relaxed with a wide-eyed look of wonder. 'The snake is not slimy', they will often say – 'It's very smooth and warm'.

4 Snakes: inside and out

Close your eyes, place your hands over your ears, join your legs together and move on the floor on your belly ... now you can imagine how hard it would be for a snake to survive in the wild, to chase and capture food, and then to swallow it without being able to shred it or cut it into pieces. It cannot hear danger and it is difficult for it to run away.

Snakes cannot regulate their own body temperature – their temperature is regulated by the environment. A snake, therefore, has a very limited activity cycle and is at the mercy of weather and climate more so than other animal groups. During winter or in cold weather when they are deprived of warmth, snakes become inactive.

The Scrub or Amethystine Python is one of Australia's largest pythons. Image: John Weigel

Snake families in Australia

Group	Family	Number of species
Blind snakes	Typhlopidae	43
File snakes	Acrochordidae	2
Pythons	Boidae	14
Colubrid snakes	Colubridae	11
Venomous (elapid) snakes	Elapidae	123

Q Can I tell a venomous snake from a harmless one by its shape or colour?

A On your life, NO! There are numerous examples of colour variations, mimicry and species that look very similar to the untrained eye. All snakes should be treated as venomous until proven otherwise.

The Keelback is harmless. Image: Lyall Naylor

The Rough-scaled Snake is potentially dangerous. Image: Martin Baxter

Snakes can be large, small, thick-bodied or long, slender and very graceful. Some snakes have heavily armoured skin; others have rough, coarse skin, but they are not slimy. Their scales act as a protective mechanism and allow them to move by securing purchase on the ground. The venom of elapid species is a highly modified form of saliva containing a complex system of proteins and enzymes, which is designed to immobilise their prey.

West-coast Banded Snake

Snakes have become adapted to most Australian environments. You can find snakes in alpine regions, deserts, rainforests, woodlands, grasslands and, yes, also in suburban yards.

Snakes have a variety of features that distinguish them from each other. To help identify a species, herpetologists count the number of mid-body scales or sub-caudal scales for a quick assessment. Some very obvious species require very little work to identify them. Others require careful scale counts and even inspection of the colour of their mouth to identify them accurately. In far north Queensland, Small-eyed Snakes and Slaty-grey Snakes are commonly misidentified; one is potentially dangerous while the other is harmless.

Snakes . . .

- have scales
- have no eyelids
- have no limbs such as legs or arms
- have no eardrums or ear openings and are deaf to most sounds
- have forked tongues (in lizards only goannas have forked tongues)
- rely on external sources of heat to maintain their body temperature

The Brown Tree Snake (banded form) forages along a branch in Northern Queensland.

Image: Lyall Naylor

Anatomy

Snakes have long bodies and have evolved elongated organs to fit inside their long bodies. Their stomach, liver and kidneys are all long and slender. Snakes have a three-chambered heart which is easily overtaxed when used for extended periods – for example, when fleeing from a threatening situation.

Instead of one penis, the male snake has two hemipenes. When engorged with blood they swell out of the cloaca and can be inserted into the female's cloaca one at a time. Usually both hemipenes are used during mating.

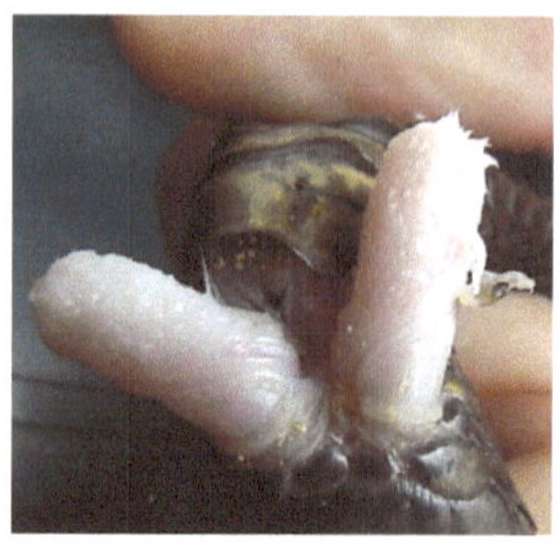

The paired hemipenes of a Lowland Copperhead.

Image: Ian Norton

Senses

Snakes have a keen sense of smell. Their increased sensitivity is due to the 'Jacobsen's Organ' located in the roof of the mouth. This organ analyses odours traced by the forked tongue.

Snakes have evolved elongated organs to fit inside their long bodies. This is a Western Brown Snake.

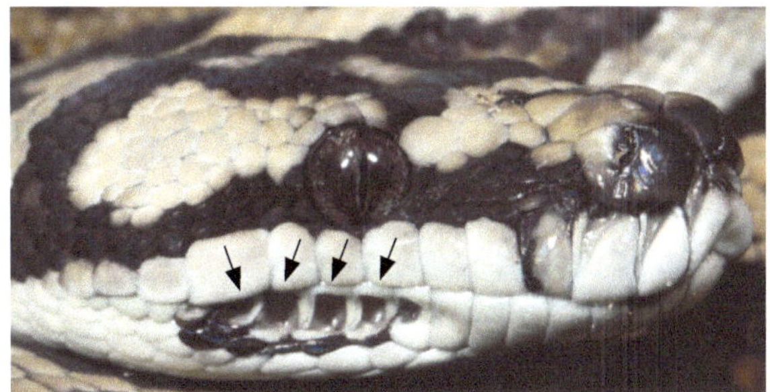
The distinctive heat sensor pits along the lower jaw of a Jungle Carpet Python.

The forked tongue in this Pygmy Mulga Snake is a highly sensitive detector. Image: Stewart MacDonald

Snakes can easily follow trails left by potential prey, such as mice, or pheromone trails left by female snakes during the breeding season.

Most pythons have heat pits on their lower jaw that effectively allows them to detect warm-blooded prey such as birds and mammals. This helps them to track their prey in foliage and within dense shrub. Some species lack these pits and tend to prey mainly on reptiles.

Compared to humans, many (but not all) snakes have relatively poor eyesight. However, when used in conjunction with their excellent sense of smell, their eyes can be used effectively. A snake's eye is covered by a specialised scale that is shed every time the snake sloughs (sheds its skin).

The nocturnal eye of a Brown Tree Snake.

Some diurnal elapids such as whip snakes and brown snakes that feed on fast-moving skinks rely largely on eyesight to chase down these agile lizards. Other species appear to have a restricted field of vision and often rely on movement – especially sudden or fast movement – to track their prey (or a possible predator).

The pupils of some nocturnal snakes close to a slit to provide better vision at night. They still need to combine all their senses – including smell and heat pits (if they have them) – to find food.

The diurnal eye-shape of a Lowland Copperhead.

The Pale-headed Snake lives in trees, under bark and inside old limbs. The scales on a snake's belly are attached to muscles which can act independently, allowing it to grip uneven surfaces. Image: John Weigel

Movement

Instead of legs snakes have lots of belly (ventral) scales attached to muscles which all can act independently to grip uneven surfaces and provide traction. This enables a snake to travel very effectively over the ground. Lateral undulation is the most common method of movement – the snake's body flicks into loops, while the last loops connect and push against any irregularities on the ground.

Some snakes can travel at around 8–10 km/hour, but most are much slower. So a snake cannot actually chase you and keep up with you. In a small, confined space a few species such as taipans and brown snakes are highly manoeuvrable.

Fangs and venom

The fangs of most venomous snakes are long and thin, hollow and have a bevelled tip. Like a syringe, these fangs have evolved to deliver a liquid (venom) under pressure from the venom glands. Hence the venom can be delivered quickly in a rapid bite. These snakes are referred to as proteroglyphs (which translates as 'front-fanged'). The fangs are replaced in cycles throughout the snake's life, with an adjacent fang ready to slot into place once the existing fang has reached the end of its cycle and falls out.

The venom of a Chappell Island Tiger Snake, secreted from its venom glands passes through its fangs. Image: John Weigel

Venom is the fluid which is secreted from the venom glands and delivered down an enclosed venom canal on the leading edge of the fang. The main effect of the venom is to immobilise the snake's prey while it also helps in digestion and possibly the preservation of food.

The venom is manufactured and stored in venom glands which are sometimes visible as noticeable swellings on either side of the head behind the eyes. The amount of venom stored fluctuates considerable between seasons, frequency of feeding, snake species, age and size of individual snakes. Some snake species, notably the Mulga Snakes and the Coastal Taipan, have a very large venom capacity. Others have very small yet powerfully toxic venom, for example, the Eastern Brown Snake.

The fangs of a Mulga Snake (left) are modest in size (4–6 mm), when compared with those of the Gaboon Viper (55 mm), found in equatorial Africa (right).

Image: Brian Bush

Blind Snakes (Family: Typhlopidae)

Blind Snakes are harmless – they have small mouths and can not bite people. They have glossy armour-like scales, very small eyes and subterranean habits. With very short, pointed tails, they are like large worms yet their forked tongue reveals them as snakes. They are rarely encountered except when uncovered through excavation, inside compost heaps or gardens. Sometimes seen on rainy nights when they emerge and move about, they appear to feed solely on the eggs of termites and ants. Image: John Weigel

Feeding

What do snakes eat and how can they possibly get food? Snakes have a specialised jaw with elastic ligaments that enable the lower jaw to expand to cope with larger food items. Most feed infrequently and rely on substantial meals to fulfil their requirements of growth and reproduction. Smaller or juvenile elapid snakes may feed more frequently than larger snakes.

All species have strategies and mechanisms for foraging and capturing their prey. Active foragers take significant risks in the open, regardless of whether it is day or night. Usually they are fast moving or camouflaged to reduce the risk of predation. They will also have defence mechanisms for confrontations with predators.

Tiger snakes make use of long grass to keep concealed as much as possible while poking their heads into suitable gaps, holes or inside logs. Brown snakes will forage widely looking in holes around shrubs, through grass tussocks and in gardens trying to flush out skinks or find mouse burrows. They rely on their speed not only to catch prey but to avoid conflict. Given the size of a taipan it seems remarkable that they are rarely spotted or confronted when foraging. Perhaps their excellent eyesight not only helps when foraging but also keeps them out of sight.

Black snakes and tiger snakes prey on frogs, such as this Green and Gold Bell Frog.

Many species, especially the large Australian elapids, prey on frogs. Black snakes and tiger snakes eat a lot of frogs, but not so much brown snakes, and taipans not at all. Even arid zone snakes will prey on frogs during times when they are plentiful. Cane Toads can adversely affect some frog predators in northern Australia, in particular Red-bellied Black Snakes and other opportunistic predators such as death adders and the Mulga Snake.

This Death Adder is making a meal of a mouse. Image: Ken Griffiths

This juvenile Diamond Python is constricting a skink. Lizards are an important source of food for many species. Image: John Weigel

Lizards are an important source of food for some smaller elapids and the juveniles of many snake species. Small skinks play an essential role in the growth of a large proportion of elapids, colubrids and pythons. Black-headed Pythons often take large dragons, skinks and even medium sized monitor lizards, while brown snakes and copperheads also prey on blue-tongue lizards.

Carpet pythons, the Scrub Python, the Brown Tree Snake, the Mulga Snake and the Eastern Tiger Snake commonly prey on birds, either nestlings or adults. In built-up areas, pet birds in cages are particularly vulnerable.

Small mammals are part of the diet of many common species. Carpet snakes, Scrub Pythons and the Mulga Snake play a role in keeping rats down. Brown snakes, tiger snakes and the Red-bellied Black Snake are drawn to regions of mouse plagues. Bats, bandicoots, antechinus and other small macropods are all common prey for a number of different species.

This Brown Tree Snake is eating a bat at the entrance of a cave in north Queensland. Image: Kelvin Marshall

This Brisbane Carpet Python has ambushed an Australian Magpie. Image: Rebecca Cockburn

While largely sensationalised, it remains a regular event that Scrub Pythons take wallabies, bettongs, possums and sometimes small domestic pet dogs and cats. Media reports often depict the swollen body that includes the recent meal! Scrub Pythons, Olive Pythons and very large carpet pythons can take some large prey which allows them to subsist for months.

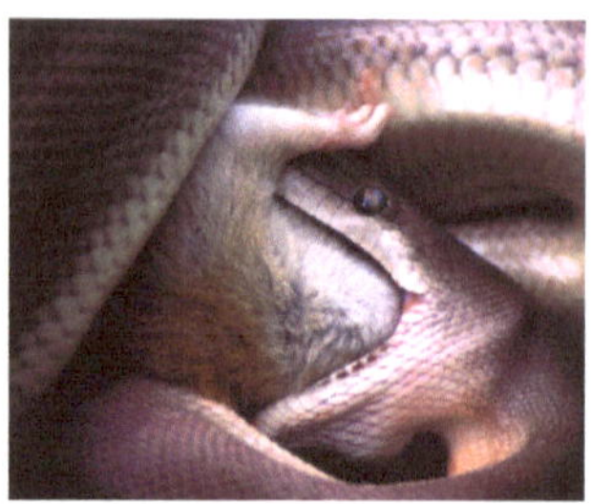

This Olive Python is feeding on a rat.

After feeding, snakes need to maintain their body temperature in order to aid and, in some cases, speed up digestion. Sometimes snakes that have eaten a very large meal can be vulnerable to predation or be killed by an irate house owner. The snake's stomach can be greatly distended with large prey, which, as it breaks down, moves further along the intestinal tract. Digestion may take up to a week or more depending on the size of the snake, its behaviour, the air temperature, and the prey type.

This Olive Python has a large wallaby to digest. Image: Ken Griffith

Q Can I use a 'slough' of a snake to identify it?

A It is possible – it can depend on the age of the shed skin and if it's intact. Sometimes you can even tell what sex the snake is!

This Yellow-faced Whip Snake is in the process of shedding its skin. Image: John Weigel

Sloughing

Snakes shed their skin as they grow, and this is sometimes a dangerous period for a snake. The outer layer of the skin will separate from the inner layer, which is aided by a milky substance that lubricates and facilitates the sloughing process. When freshly shed, the sloughed skin is soft and quite moist but may dry very quickly and after a week will become brittle and fragment easily. Naturally, younger snakes may slough more regularly than adults whose growth is less pronounced. If you find a snake slough, it does not necessarily mean the snake is still in the area.

This Collared Whip Snake has sloughed off its skin in single piece. Image: Lyall Naylor

Behaviour

Snakes have evolved to be secretive and shy. They are very selective about the time they spend foraging and try to conserve energy as much as possible. Many species of snakes openly forage for their prey, investigating rocks, holes or under bushes.

Death adders and some pythons rely on ambush behaviour to catch their prey as it walks or flies past. They move only when conditions suit or perhaps hunger forces them to choose another spot. Other snakes live underground, in ant or termite tunnels, or beneath the surface in sand. Males of nearly every species become more active and range more widely during the breeding season.

Some species rely on having an abundance of trees and tree hollows, some specialise in areas with rocks and boulders, while others are largely dependent on rivers, streams, creeks, ponds or swamps.

The type of habitat will often dictate which animals you will find in your area. Rural or what are called 'disturbed areas' also favour certain species of snakes. For example, changes to the land by humans tend to make the Eastern Brown Snake more abundant – especially with the introduction of its favourite food source – the House Mouse. The Coastal Carpet Python has adapted to living in the roof of some Queensland houses, where it thrives on warm conditions during winter and plentiful prey like rats and possums.

Over the last 200 years, sudden and drastic changes to the environment have been devastating for many of Australia's animals. In some cases, snakes (like all the other fauna) have had to adapt very quickly to new prey species (introduced rodents or birds) as well as to new predator species (cats and foxes).

Normally nocturnal, death adders can sometimes be seen sheltering in leaf litter or moving to a new ambush location.

Image: John Weigel

Reproduction

In the southern part of Australia, many reptiles are influenced by the spring months to become active and begin to reproduce. Males often mate with females in early spring, yet the females retain the sperm until they ovulate which could be two months later.

Mating begins first with courtship, in which the male sniffs and rubs his body alongside the female. This develops into twitching and raking (in pythons using the spurs). Mating can go for hours and days as the male follows the female around. Death adders can often be seen copulating in daylight hours. Pairs of snakes are commonly seen in spring e.g. elapids and in dry periods in the north e.g. Scrub Pythons.

The Diamond Python can form large aggregations in trees where up to a dozen snakes may share partners,

Mating snakes, such as these two Green Pythons, adopt a relaxed side-by-side posture.

Image: Byron Manning

Two male tiger snakes in ritual combat. Image: Ian Norton

quite a sight to see! Some species aggregate in winter and such aggregations are believed to revolve around mating as well, e.g. Small-eyed Snake, Green Tree Snake, Little Whip Snake, blind snakes.

Males in a number of species, both harmless and venomous, do 'ritual combat'. This involves entwining their lengths and using the head to suppress the head of the rival. To the casual observer it looks like mating!

After mating, a female may store sperm for up to several months until her follicles enlarge and are fertilised. The follicles develop into embryos or eggs. In the southern states of Australia snakes mostly mate in the spring and the young are born or hatch in late summer to early autumn, while many northern species rely on seasonal changes – the dry or wet seasons – to stimulate breeding. Some cold temperate southern species like tigers and copperheads mate in autumn and can mate again in early spring.

These python eggs are soft when first laid then harden with exposure to air.

A Dwarf-crowned Snake laying eggs in a damp nest of moss.
Image: John Weigel

Baby Black-headed Pythons, emerging from eggs. Image: Lyall Naylor

Collett's Snake, a member of the black snake family, is found in inland Queensland. This gravid female will bask in the sun to help incubate her eggs before laying them in a burrow or under a log. Image: Stewart McDonald

The site a female chooses for her young to be born plays a big role in its chances of survival. Good mothers live near waterways or in skink-infested rocky outcrops to give the young snakes the best chance. Urban gardens, too, can have a suitable food source nearby.

Some female snake species lay eggs: others give birth to live young. Typically all pythons, tree snakes and some venomous snakes lay eggs, while many venomous snakes and sea snakes have live young which usually will emerge from embryo sacs. Eastern Brown Snakes often lay eggs under concrete driveways or inside pool walls to help incubate the eggs and be close to a good food source.

Young snakes need to find food and avoid being eaten by other snakes, birds and mammals. They ultimately rely on camouflage to hide and their small size enables them to fit into small spaces and prey on small skinks and frogs.

Red-bellied Black Snakes are diurnal and most commonly encountered in spring when males are actively searching for mates.

Seasonal behaviour

Snakes are known as 'ectothermic' animals which means they rely on external sources for heat and cannot perform many normal functions without being sufficiently warm. They try to maintain what is called a 'preferred body temperature' – this is the temperature the snake needs to be in order to search for, prey on and digest food. Some snakes are specifically adapted to cooler regions and others to arid or dry regions.

Spring months are largely responsible for large movements of male snakes, which travel around following female pheromone trails. Foraging is very important at this time, too. Snakes have to get off to a good start after winter, with plenty of basking behaviour and foraging for food. Late spring often sees a large amount of roadkill as snakes start to move distances.

In the north of Australia, monsoonal weather plays an important role in snake behaviour. During the wet season, many species breed and become more active while food is plentiful. The sudden growth of grass and other vegetation allows snakes to forage mostly protected from sight. Humid nights with low moons typically encourage plenty of movement from both nocturnal and diurnal snakes. Because the day can be too hot, some snakes switch to foraging during the early hours of the evening e.g. Mulga Snakes, Western Brown Snakes, tiger snakes and copperheads.

In the south, during the heat of summer, species such as the Eastern Tiger Snake and the Lowland Copperhead become active after dusk, to prevent overheating. Eastern Tiger Snakes are particularly active on humid nights in January and February during storms.

Blind snakes emerge on warm nights but quickly return to their refuge underground.

Defence

As part of their defence, snakes use a variety of threat displays. These range from rearing of the head, flattening of the body (to make it look larger), continual or explosive hissing, mock strikes, an open mouth and, as a last resort, a bite.

With its 'flared hood' and hissing loudly, this Mulga Snake is giving a serious and clear signal.

Image: John Weigel

This Common Death Adder is making use of leaf litter to conceal itself from would-be predators. Image: Martin Baxter

When direct confrontation looks imminent, most snakes will seek an escape route and will flee. They have a good sense of direction and memory of shelter locations. A quick flick and often an observer just sees them slide down a burrow. In my experience, brown snakes will move when approached within 5 m, but with Eastern Tiger Snakes the distance is usually around 1.5 m. Why is this? Brown snakes are built for speed and their eyesight is more acute, so they avoid confrontations. Tiger snakes, on the other hand, are often active at relatively low air temperatures that restrict their ability to move quickly.

Quite a few species rely on camouflage. The ability of some species to blend in with their surroundings is quite remarkable – and acts as a protection for them.

A Common Tree Snake coiled in a vine thicket or a Diamond Python in a tree in a yard can be overlooked day after day. Only a movement of the snake or the call of agitated birds will sometimes reveal its presence.

A death adder is remarkable in its ability to remain motionless for large periods of time, coiled in leaf litter or in sand with just its head sticking out! A bite from this species occurs when the person inadvertently steps on it or places their hands on it during a field trip or when gardening.

A West-coast Banded Snake in a tight coil to protect its head from attack.

Virtually all snakes have stinky anal glands which presumably act as part of their defence.

Semi-aquatic snakes or those associated with water (such as Red-bellied Black Snakes and Keelbacks) defend themselves by escaping into a river, dam or pond.

Some species of burrowing snakes and smaller elapids sometimes protect their head by placing it inside their coiled-up body. Just which predator this technique would work against is not really known.

The Bandy Bandy in an unusual defensive hoop. This snake feeds on blind snakes, and is only occasionally seen at night.

Image: Stewart McDonald

5 Living with snakes

Pythons

Australia has a wonderful diversity of pythons. Some are terrestrial (living on land), some are arboreal (living in trees) and some are semi-aquatic (spending some of their time in water).

Pythons usually have large heads, thin necks and stout bodies. Nearly all have heat pits on their lower jaw that help them to detect warm-blooded prey at night. Members of the genus *Aspidites*, including the Black-headed Python and Woma, do not have these heat pits; these two snakes specialise in eating reptiles, including venomous snakes.

The females of all species lay eggs and incubate them by coiling around and 'shivering' the eggs, keeping them at a constant temperature. This is about as maternal as snakes go.

Pythons are attracted to houses and rural properties because of the range of artificial shelter sites and the easy-to-get-at pests and native species, often in abundance. They may take up residence in a roof space, while ornamental birds, chickens and (occasionally) domestic cats or dogs offer a quick and potentially long-lasting meal. Pythons are patient predators often waiting a month or two for a large meal.

Carpet pythons are arboreal and are the most common python seen around residences in Australia. They occur in all the main cities except Melbourne, Adelaide and Hobart – pet pythons excluded. Carpet pythons have a diverse range of colourations and patterns.

All pythons are harmless yet they have very sharp, recurved teeth that can cause some local damage. Generally all python bites will need medical advice and all snakebites should be treated as venomous until proved otherwise.

The rarely seen Woma is a python without heat pits. It is found in arid Australia.

The small Jungle Carpet Python is found at higher altitudes in northern Queensland. It is usually arboreal and active at night.

The **Jungle Carpet Python**, *Morelia spilota cheynei,* has a maximum size of about 1.2 m and is often spectacularly marked with 'black and gold' colouration. It tends to prey on birds and smaller mammals. This sub-species is largely restricted to the tablelands of North Queensland from Townsville to around Cape Tribulation. It usually occurs in rainforest regions associated with Scrub Pythons. Most Jungle Carpet Pythons are quite 'bitey' and wild specimens need to be handled with care.

The **Brisbane** (or **Coastal**) **Carpet Python,** *Morelia spilota mcdowelli*, has a highly variable pattern and is the largest carpet python sub-species with some specimens nearly 3 m in length. With a coastal range from northern New South Wales through Brisbane to south of Cairns, it is the most common 'nuisance' snake in Brisbane and coastal Queensland. In Brisbane, these pythons can over-winter in the roof space. They will exit usually after the spring weather and night time temperatures increase. They will prey on birds, rats, possums, cats (pet and feral)

Harmless but a bite may need treatment

The Brisbane (or Coastal) Carpet Python may reach nearly 3 m in length. This is the New South Wales form.

and sometimes will take larger birds such as ducks and chickens. It reaches 2.5 m in length.

The **Murray–Darling Carpet Python,** *Morelia spilota metcalfei,* is also known as the Victorian or Inland Carpet Python. It is another smaller species (average size around 1.5 m) that favours River Red Gum woodlands especially where they intersect with rocky regions. This species is commonly found in the eaves of houses in rural districts. It can live in roof spaces and barn rafters.

The **Western Carpet Python** *Morelia spilota imbricata,* is common in some regions of Perth and some offshore islands (e.g. Garden Island). Similar in habit to the other carpet pythons, it is common in farms, houses and out-buildings. It can take up residence in roof spaces and feeds on rats, birds and mice.

The **Diamond Python**, *Morelia spilota spilota,* is Sydney's most common python and is quite common along the coast of Eastern Australia from northern New South Wales to Gippsland, Victoria. A very gentle species,

The Western Carpet Python may be encountered around the Perth region. Image: Brian Bush

it inhabits escarpments and rocky woodlands where it overwinters in depressions or cavities in sandstone or granite outcrops, particularly on north-facing slopes.

On winter and spring days of suitably warmish weather, it will bask with most of its coils exposed to direct sunlight. It becomes active in spring and can often be seen in large aggregations for mating purposes. It is commonly seen in roof spaces and sheds of rural and suburban residences. The pattern of this python allows it to blend magnificently within the shade of trees – often homeowners are not even aware of its presence!

The Murray–Darling Python is also known as the Inland Carpet Python.

The beautiful Diamond Python is common in sandstone, heathland and forested regions of coastal south-eastern Australia.

The **Northern Carpet Python**, *Morelia spilota variegata,* (also called the Darwin Carpet Python) is a stout sub-species that is common around Darwin residences. It is a common predator of possums, rats, birds and fruit bats, but will also raid aviaries for chickens, ducks or ornamental species.

The **Centralian Carpet Python**, *Morelia spilota bredii,* is an attractive species with striking caramel brown patterns on a cream body. It is common along the watercourses of central Australia where it shelters in the hollows and trunks of old trees. It is often captured around Alice Springs where it is drawn to pet birds and rodents.

The Northern Carpet Python is found around residences in Darwin.

The attractively coloured Centralian Carpet Python is about 2 m in length. It may be found in Alice Springs.

The **Scrub Python** (also known as the Amethystine Python or 'Scrubbie'), *Morelia kinghorni,* is a regular, 'nuisance' snake in Far North Queensland. It is Australia's largest python, with a recorded length of 5.5 m. It preys on macropods, especially wallabies, but it will often feed on fruit bats, bettongs, birds, bandicoots and large rodents. It can be seen in the canopy of large trees or basking/ resting on very large ferns in dense rainforest. The Scrub Python will forage around properties, looking for easy prey such as chickens, ducks, pet cats and ornamental birds; also rabbits and rats. It frequents roof spaces where it will spend the dry season, taking any available possums and rats. It may been seen crossing the road at night and care should be taken to avoid injuring it. The Scrub Python should not be handled or approached as it has quite an injurious bite and powerful coils.

The Scrub Python has powerful coils and a nasty bite. It is a regular 'nuisance' snake in Far North Queensland. This specimen is from Cape Tribulation, Queensland.

Image: Lyall Naylor

Children's Python is common around Darwin. It may be seen crossing roads and is active at night around residences. When inactive, it may be found under woodpiles or corrugated iron.

image: Stewart McDonald.

Children's Python, *Antaresia childreni,* is usually associated with the Top End tropics; however, it also occurs in some moister locations and is common around Darwin and some rural and outback communities of the Top End. A gentle python, it usually forages around for mice and lizards. It grows to about 1 m in length.

The **Spotted Python**, *Antaresia maculosa,* is associated with moist forest and woodlands more likely to be found along the eastern side of Australia. It is sometimes found under fallen timber, iron sheets and other debris around properties. It grows to about 1 m in length.

The Spotted Python, less than 1 m in length is found in the coastal regions of Queensland and northern New South Wales.

Stimson's Python is similar to the Spotted Python. It is about 1 m in length. Image: Steven Cook

Stimson's Python, *Antaresia stimsoni*, is similar to the Spotted Python but is found more inland in Queensland, New South Wales, Northern Territory and Western Australia. It is sometimes seen around properties preying on pet birds. It is less than 1 m in length.

The **Black-headed Python**, *Aspidites melanocephalus*, is a very striking and easily identified python, although it bears some resemblance to the Western Brown Snake. This python inhabits the northern parts of Australia, largely confined to the humid and sub-humid woodlands and plains. The snake lacks the heat pits that most pythons have, this explains its preference for reptilian prey, but it

The Black-headed Python is sometimes confused with the Western Brown Snake. It is usually between 1.5 and 2 m in length.

Image: Stewart McDonald

will also take small mammals and sometimes birds. Up to 2.5 m in length with a very black head and irregular banding, this stunning snake usually has a threat display that's worth heeding. The Black-headed Python means trouble for other snakes, as it will take any snake – including venomous ones.

The **Water Python**, *Liasis fuscus*, is associated with waterways, particularly billabongs and floodplains and may be seen around Darwin. It commonly feeds on plains rats and waterbirds, and may be seen at night crossing roads or foraging in yards for mammals or birds (including pets). Snakes from the Northern Territory are more inclined to bite when handled, while Queensland and Western Australian populations are more reserved in temperament. The Water Python is commonly confused with the highly dangerous Mulga Snake.

The semi-aquatic Water Python is stoutly built, usually about 1.2 m in length.

Image: Stewart McDonald.

Harmless but large specimens cause concern

The Olive Python can grow to more than 5 m in length.

Image: Chris Pederby

The **Olive Python**, *Liasis olivaceus*, is a very large python that is mainly associated with inland regions of Australia from Queensland across the Top End including Darwin through the Kimberley region of Western Australia. Smaller individuals are often confused with the dangerously venomous Mulga Snake. This python can feed on large prey including small macropods and may be seen moving on roads at night or foraging around residences looking for possums, pets (including cats and dogs), rats and birds. It rarely climbs – it is primarily terrestrial and nocturnal.

Non-venomous and rear-fanged venomous snakes

The Colubridae is a unique family whose members include the rear-fanged Brown Tree Snake, the harmless Common Tree Snake, Keelbacks and the Slaty-grey Snake. The colubrids form a diverse group that is widely distributed in other continents but poorly represented in Australia.

The **Brown Tree Snake**, *Boiga irregularis,* is very common around properties in some parts of its distribution e.g. Darwin, Cairns, Brisbane and small towns of coastal Queensland. Several colour forms exist, from weakly reddish-brown to strongly banded red-brown on creamy white. It is usually seen going after captive birds, rodents, frogs, lizards and bats.

The Brown Tree Snake is also known as the Dolls-eye Snake or Night Tiger. Large specimens can grow to 2 m.

Bites readily, mildly venomous with local effects

Bites readily, mildly venomous with local effects

This form of the Brown Tree Snake is found in New South Wales.

Image: John Weigel

Arboreal and nocturnal, the Brown Tree Snake sometimes moves around the rafters in roof spaces and ceilings. It tends to strike and sometimes bite if it is handled or harassed. Its venom, injected through its rear fangs, is weak but medical attention is still required. The Brown Tree Snake is commonly seen around aviaries and inside small birdcages preying on captive birds.

The **Common Tree Snake**, *Dendrelaphis punctulata,* is common in eastern and northern Australia, from Gippsland, Victoria, right through Sydney, Brisbane, Townsville and Cairns and across the Top End to Darwin. It grows to about 1 m but is quite thin. Often seen around the house by day foraging for frogs, geckos and skinks, the Common Tree Snake is harmless and easily frightened. There are five common colour forms of this species – light green, blue, dark green, gold and brown.

Image: Ken Griffiths

The Common Tree Snake is about 1 m in length and is active during the day. It has several colour forms. The typical green form (top) is common in Sydney and through to Brisbane and some parts of Northern Queensland. The blue form (middle left) is locally common in some parts of Queensland; the golden form (middle right) is from northern Australia and often seen in the Darwin area; dark green form (bottom left) is from Northern Queensland.

Harmless

The **Keelback** or **Freshwater Snake,** *Tropidonophis mairii,* is a small, harmless species, associated with waterways, rivers, creeks, swamps and ponds. It is active by day and is common in north-eastern and northern Australia. It is locally common around household ponds, farm dams and larger water where it forages for frogs or basks in the sun. Keelbacks specialise in eating frogs and will also eat small metamorphling Cane Toads, and occasionally an adult toad.

The small and slender Keelback is active during the day. It has several colour variations.

Images: Lyall Naylor

The Keelback looks very similar to the dangerously venomous Rough-scaled Snake. It is small and slender, usually only about 60 cm in length. If threatened, it usually makes for shelter and, if handled, it may bite or shed its tail. There are several colour variations.

Harmless but can become agitated and bite

The **Slaty-grey Snake**, *Stegonotus cucullatus* is often grey to dark grey (almost black) above and pale white or cream underneath. Specimens can grow to 1.2 m. It is common in some areas of the Top End, foraging around properties looking for food, especially mice and small pet birds. The Slaty-grey Snake is very active and can climb readily. If harassed, it releases a strong, distasteful odour. It is also quite pugnacious – if handled it may thrash and bite, providing a nasty experience. All bites should be treated as medically significant (due to similarity to other venomous species).

The relatively harmless Slaty-grey Snake is often mistaken for the potentially dangerously venomous Small-eyed Snake.

The Slaty-grey Snake is usually about 1–1.2 m in length. Mostly terrestrial, it will occasionally climb. In Queensland, it is commonly confused with the venomous Small-eyed Snake.

Image: Lyall Naylor

Front-fanged venomous snakes

This family of snakes, Elapidae, includes both land and sea venomous snakes. They have evolved venom (and the apparatus to deliver it) primarily in order to subdue their prey and to assist in the breakdown of their food.

Elapid snakes exist in a wide range of habitats and are mostly active during the day. Most feed on lizards, frogs, or mammals, although some are more specialised in their choice of prey – for example, blind snakes or lizard eggs. They can vary in size from 10 cm to over 3 m. Only 25 or so species are considered potentially fatal, the other species have weak, unknown or localised effects.

Some elapid snakes lay eggs (oviparous), some bear live young (viviparous) while others bear their young still enclosed in a membrane (ovoviviparous). Most sea snakes give birth in the water, while the land elapids will lay eggs in burrows, under warm shelter sites like rocks or use logs etc. There is no maternal care and young disperse to fend for themselves.

Death adders are highly distinctive with their heavily banded stout bodies and broad heads. With their effective camouflage, they make excellent ambush predators waiting for unsuspecting prey to go past. They invariably bury themselves in sand, leaf litter or among dense vegetation, leaving just their head and their 'caudal lure' exposed. They wriggle the lure in order to entice birds or hungry mammals to investigate.

Most cases of adder bites are from stepping on a death adder due to their ambush nature – they rarely move even when approached closely. Relatively large fangs and an incredible strike (the fastest in Australian snakes) ensure they maximise their chance of dinner! Their diet consists of lizards, small mammals, birds and frogs.

Death adders are nocturnal, but can sometimes be seen during the day after light showers sitting above leaf litter or moving slowly to a new ambush location.

The endangered Broad-headed Snake gives birth to live young.

Image: John Weigel

The Southern (or Common) Death Adder grows to about 75 cm. It has a stout body and arrow-like head, and has several colour variations. Image: Stewart McDonald

Most commonly, however, they are seen at night especially if there is no moon and the conditions are warm with some light rain.

Gardeners can disturb adders when raking or moving garden mulch or leaf litter. On coastlines death adders have been removed from clumps of washed-up seaweed. Bushwalkers can sometimes step on adders when off track in bushland. Likewise, on warm evenings adders can be seen moving across roads, through yards and in natural habitats. The protection of thick boots and socks will help protect many from severe envenoming.

Their large fangs and a good amount (70–95 mg) of venom stored in their glands create a major hazard for people if bitten. The venom is powerfully neurotoxic and acts rapidly; it may cause paralysis and eventually death if untreated. Clinical signs of envenoming are drooping eyelids, nausea, vomiting, abdominal pain, diarrhoea, dizziness, collapse or convulsions, and breathing and speech difficulties. Most bites require death adder antivenom.

The Desert Death Adder inhabits very arid regions with hot summers and cold winters.

Image: Brian Bush

The **Southern (or Common) Death Adder**, *Acanthophis antarcticus*, has the largest distribution of all adders. It is found in eastern Australia, but rarely in Victoria. Its range extends across South Australia to southern Western Australia. There are some colour variations – greyish, reddish and brownish, heavily and thickly banded.

The **Northern Death Adder**, *Acanthophis praelongus,* is common across the north of Australia, but is under threat by the Cane Toad invasion. The Northern Death Adder is lighter coloured than the southern species. It is occasionally seen at night around residences in Cairns and Darwin, especially on warm evenings when there are dramatic changes in the weather such as cold fronts or tropical storms.

The **Desert Death Adder,** *Acanthophis pyrrhus,* lives in the arid regions of central and western Australia among spinifex grass and rocky outcrops. It is commonly seen in and around Alice Springs although it rarely presents a problem to residents.

Northern Death Adder.

Dangerously venomous

Copperheads

All copperheads are dangerously venomous, but display more threat than bite. They are arguably one of the most inoffensive venomous snakes in Australia, and are commonly confused with Red-bellied Black Snakes and Eastern Brown Snake. They eat mainly lizards, frogs and snakes (including other copperheads).

Copperheads are common around residences near Melbourne and in higher altitude rural and coastal Victoria across to Mt Gambier, South Australia. They grow to about 1.5 m. There are various colour forms: golden brown, dark brown (appears black), reddish-brown and muddy brown. The typical brown form is usually mistaken for a brown snake. Sometimes a faint to prominent line appears along the middle of the snake's body.

Copperheads have a threat display that includes a loud burst of hissing together with the flattening of the entire body and the odd mock strike. While usually all bluff, copperheads do occasionally bite when extremely over-

The Lowland Copperhead is sometimes mistaken for the Red-bellied Black Snake.

The Lowland Copperhead grows to over 1 m in length. Active by day, it may be encountered on warm nights.

Dangerously venomous

The Highland Copperhead is found in the sub-alpine regions of eastern Australia. Image: Ken Griffiths

stressed by heat or agitation from injury, but this is quite rare. Most suspected bites are the result of a closed mouth strike. Their bite is regarded as medically significant and may be treated with tiger snake monovalent antivenom.

The **Lowland Copperhead**, *Austrelaps superbus*, is the most frequently encountered species seen regularly in Tasmania and south-eastern Melbourne, but less so in other regions. They are mostly active in spring especially on low wind, sunny days, with temperatures of 17–25°C. The males are commonly encountered searching for food or females. In summer, heat stress is a common cause for copperheads to venture indoors to escape the heat.

The **Highland Copperhead**, *Austrelaps ramsayi*, is more common in the higher altitudes of sub-alpine regions of eastern Victoria and New South Wales. Like most copperheads the Highland Copperhead is associated with water, and may be found in moist habitats in woodlands and grasslands. Highland Copperheads have been seen basking on sunny days in winter surrounded by snow!

A black form of the Lowland Copperhead from Tasmania.

Image: Ian Norton

Tiger snakes

The **Tiger Snake**, *Notechis scutatus*, has a wide distribution that extends from south Western Australia, through South Australia, Victoria, coastal New South Wales, and into south-eastern Queensland, with isolated populations around Brisbane. The species has successfully adapted to the cooler climates of high altitude mountain ranges up to 900 m, and has colonised numerous islands across south-eastern and Western Australia.

Tiger snakes have achieved notoriety in Australia due to their frequent bite history, close proximity to cities and 'cobra-like' stance. Typically, adults have a stout body with square to triangular-shaped heads in large specimens. They usually have distinct bands but their colouration is very diverse – including grey, brown, orange red, blue-grey, light honey-brown, dark brown (almost black) and yellowish. Their belly is usually pale cream, white or greyish. Unbanded specimens are common in most states, but more so in southern

Defensive behaviour in a tiger snake from Launceston, Tasmania.

The Western Tiger Snake is commonly seen around Perth and south-western Australia.

An Eastern Tiger Snake, Mornington Peninsula, Victoria.

An unbanded orange form of the Eastern Tiger Snake from South Australia. Image: Peter Mirtchin.

An Eastern Tiger Snake from Underwood, Tasmania. Image: Simon Fearn

regions such as Tasmania. An unbanded tiger snake may be confused with a Lowland Copperhead or (on the mainland) an Eastern Brown Snake. Chappell Island has the largest tiger snakes – some are nearly 2 m in length and 3 kg in weight. The largest nuisance snake removed in Melbourne was 1.2 m and 1.5 kg in weight.

Tiger snakes prefer moist environments where frogs are plentiful. However, they can be found some distance from water in grasslands, woodlands, basalt plains, riverine woodlands and sclerophyll forests especially with bracken fern understorey. While some tiger snakes survive human-made changes to landscapes, their numbers have appeared to dwindle as frog populations have declined. Farm dams, human-made lakes and introduced vegetation have afforded some protection, but the major tiger snake populations of the large river systems (e.g. the River Murray) have dramatically declined and appear in serious trouble.

The prey of tiger snakes includes not only frogs but lizards, nestling birds (starlings, willie wagtails, noisy miners and even muttonbirds), small mammals (antechinus, mice, rats and even small rabbits, rarely). They will forage slowly through vegetation, small trees, along rooftops and inside the roof space. While not elegant climbers they do achieve results by preying on nestlings and rats in the ceilings of residences. Tiger snakes will probe holes, cracks in timber, rocks and other spaces to find resting frogs or lizards or mouse burrows. They are fond of sheltering under iron sheets, fallen timber, under rocks, within dense grasses and especially within introduced ivy and agapanthus clumps. Rabbit burrows make great winter holes. While snakes use shelter sites around properties they rarely remain long.

The author catching a Chappell Island Tiger Snake.

Chappell Island Tiger Snake.

The Eastern Tiger Snake has faint bands.

Tiger snakes like to lie in the sun, and have a habit of basking on footpaths, bush tracks, roads and in gardens. When alerted, the snake invariably raises its head aloft and flatten its hood while hissing. It will move away from the intruder and try to escape down a hole or inside vegetation or a hollow log. If you interfere with it, it may lunge at you and, if harassed further, attempt to bite. Pet dogs often mouth tiger snakes, with fatal outcomes. It is not unusual for tiger snakes to face off a dog in a 'Mexican standoff' for hours, until the owner comes home.

Eastern Tiger Snakes are commonly confused with:

NSW	Rough-scaled Snakes, Stephens Banded Snake, (unbanded snakes) Eastern Brown Snakes, Lowland Copperheads
QLD	Rough-scaled Snakes, Stephens Banded Snake, (unbanded snakes) Eastern Brown Snakes, Keelbacks
SA	(Unbanded snakes) Eastern Brown Snakes, Lowland Copperheads
TAS	(Unbanded snakes) Lowland Copperheads
VIC	(Unbanded snakes) Eastern Brown Snakes, Lowland Copperheads

Taipans

Before the 1950s, a bite from a **Taipan**, *Oxyuranus scutellatus*, was invariably fatal. In Far North Queensland, the taipan achieved a reputation as 'The Cane Field Killer'. However, the taipan has very good eyesight and quick reflexes that enable it to escape any potential confrontation very rapidly, so the snake often goes unnoticed by unsuspecting people.

Taipans are very large – 2.5 m or more in length. They can raise a large proportion of their body off the ground, strike incredibly fast and accurately, then move away rapidly from the bitten person. If it is cornered or harassed, a taipan will prove to be a dangerous threat. Among all elapids this snake is truly one to treat with the utmost respect.

Taipans have developed a powerful venom that enables them to employ the 'bite and release' mode of attack on small to medium-sized mammals, especially rats. Other snakes such as tiger snakes and brown snakes bite

Taipan. Image: Peter Mirtschin

Taipan, darker phase,

Image: Lyall Naylor.

and hold on to their prey, sometimes receiving potentially fatal wounds from the prey fighting back. The taipan, however, with its powerfully neurotoxic venom, releases the bitten victim which may only get several metres from its attacker before collapsing with paralysis.

The less commonly encountered **Inland** or **Western Taipan**, *Oxyuranus microlepidotus*, has arguably the most toxic venom in the world, but really is quite a shy snake.

The taipan often uses burrows or shelters in large piles of timber or rocks, or under galvanised iron. It will forage around properties looking for food and is commonly drawn to sources of rats or bandicoots. Properties bordering on sugar cane plantations or directly to other taipan habitats are more at risk of visits and a yard clean-up is highly advisable.

The taipan is commonly confused with:

NSW	Eastern Brown Snake
NT	Northern Brown Snake, Mulga Snake
QLD	Eastern Brown Snake
WA	Northern Brown Snake, Mulga Snake

Black snakes

In Australia there are six species of black snake belonging to the genus *Pseudechis*. Only two species, the Red-bellied Black Snake and the Mulga Snake, are common. The other species have a limited or restricted outback distribution so are not often encountered.

The **Red-bellied Black Snake**, *Pseudechis porphyriacus*, is commonly found on properties in New South Wales, Queensland and rural Victoria. It usually occurs in regions with large water bodies especially rivers, creeks, some lakes and swamps. It has a glossy black dorsal surface, a distinctive pink to strong red belly, and grows to about 1.5–2 m in length.

Red-bellied Black Snakes are predominantly diurnal, but occasionally they are active at night. Although largely associated with water, they have a large home range and forage widely, often at some distance from water. They feed on frogs, lizards, other snakes (including their own species), and occasionally mice or nestlings.

The Red-bellied Black Snake is usually about 1.5 m in length, and is the most commonly encountered species of black snake. Image: Ken Griffith

The Mulga Snake (or King Brown Snake) is usually active by day, but is commonly seen at night during hot weather. It grows to 3 m.

Image: John Weigel

When threatened, a Red-bellied Black Snake will try to escape into water or some other shelter, but if harassed further will flatten its neck and arch slightly, hissing loudly. Unique within the genus, this species is ovovivaprous, with 8–15 young born in membranous sacs, in late summer.

The **Mulga Snake**, *Pseudechis australis*, is also called the **King Brown Snake**, although it should perhaps more properly be called the King Black Snake! It is a large, stout snake, about 2.5–3 m in length. It preys on pythons, other venomous snakes, monitor lizards, large dragons and skinks. Its habitats are varied – tropical forest, semi-arid and arid scrublands and grasslands. Within regions and populations its colours vary too – including light brown, olive-brown, reddish-brown or copper red. In some area, snakes may have scales edged with black, creating a reticulated appearance.

Active by both day and night, it is more often seen at night in the tropical and arid areas of Australia. The Mulga Snake used to be quite common in Darwin, but the invasion of Cane Toads has caused its numbers to drop dramatically. It is now more noticeably seen in outback and rural areas. It is occasionally seen in Alice Springs and Perth. Mulga Snakes will visit properties in search of rodents or pet birds. They will shelter in burrows, under fallen logs, in debris or rock outcrops.

The Mulga Snake has good-sized fangs and produces a large amount of venom that contains several potent toxins. A bite will cause pain and extensive swelling, which may involve much of the bitten limb; however, permanent tissue damage is rare and the swelling usually subsides in two to four days. The principal clinical problem with mulga snakebites is myolysis (skeletal-type muscle damage and breakdown), which may be severe, with potential for secondary kidney failure.

The Red-bellied Black Snake is commonly confused with:

ACT	Small–eyed Snake
NSW	Spotted Black Snake, Slaty-grey Snake, Lowland Copperhead, Small-eyed Snake
QLD	Spotted Black Snake, Slaty-grey Snake, Small-eyed Snake
SA	Peninsula or Kreftt's Tiger Snake
VIC	Lowland Copperhead, Small-eyed Snake

The Mulga Snake is commonly confused with:

NSW	Eastern Brown Snake, Southern Brown Snake
NT	Pygmy Mulga Snake, Water Python, Olive Python, Eastern Brown, Western Brown Snake, Northern Brown Snake
QLD	Pygmy Mulga Snake, Water Python, Olive Python, Coastal Taipan
SA	Peninsula Brown Snake
WA	Olive Python, Water Python, Dugite, Butler's Snake, Pygmy Mulga Snake, Western Brown Snake and Northern Brown Snake

Brown snakes

These snakes are the most dangerous in Australia. There are several species all belonging to the genus *Pseudonaja*. All eastern Australian capitals (except Hobart) have the Eastern Brown Snake; Perth has predominantly the Dugite and, to a lesser degree on the outskirts, the Western Brown Snake; and Darwin has the Northern Brown Snake. It becomes especially problematic in some rural and outback parts of Australia, where several species may occur together!

Away from towns, settlements and farms, brown snakes prey on lizards (especially skinks), snakes (including other brown snakes), occasionally birds (nestlings), frogs and small mammals. The abundant house or field mouse is its primary prey in both urban and rural environments, which has allowed for a corresponding increase in abundance of these snakes near people.

An Eastern Brown Snake in strike posture reveals its typical reddish-orange underbelly spots.

Image: Ken Griffiths

Eastern Brown Snake.

Image: Ken Griffiths

Dangerously venomous

The **Eastern Brown Snake**, *Pseudonaja textilis*, is the leading problem snake in Adelaide, and a common snake in the metropolitan areas of Melbourne, Canberra, Sydney and Brisbane. Its average length is 1.5 m, but some individuals may grow to 2 m. It is attracted to properties for mice and rats but will forage around large areas hunting for food. When cornered or provoked, it will take up a unique S-shaped defensive position with its mouth agape.

The adult Eastern Brown Snake may be brown, grey, blackish, or occasionally reddish. Juveniles may have a black head and a number of darker rings which fade as they age.

Bottom images: Ken Griffiths

Dangerously venomous

A typical banded phase of a juvenile Eastern Brown Snake from metropolitan Sydney. Its bands fade with age.

Image: John Weigel

All brown snakes lay eggs, most hatching from February through till April. These are usually laid in late spring or early summer. Brown snakes are both diurnal and nocturnal during hot weather. They tend to be extremely nervous and less inclined to tolerate direct and hostile confrontations. They do have wonderful eyesight and generally avoid people, but confrontations do occur when a snake is taken by surprise. When startled or under attack, they can be difficult to handle.

Brown snake venom is powerfully neurotoxic and also interferes with the blood's ability to clot. Bleeding in victims is often exacerbated by dilation of the blood vessels. The quicker the treatment with antivenom the better – sometimes multiple doses are required if the snake has injected a lot of venom. However, brown snakes have short fangs, and long pants, socks and good boots can help greatly in reducing the risk of a serious bite.

The **Dugite**, *Pseudonaja affinis,* is found in the coastal and nearby areas of south-west Western Australia, extending to South Australia and the southern coastal towns from Ceduna to Port Lincoln. It is common around metropolitan Perth, preying on mice and small lizards. It grows to about 1.5–2 m in length.

The Dugite varies widely in colour, with grey, olive or brown above, a dark grey throat, and a salmon or olive coloured belly. Some individuals have scattered black specks or markings.

When threatened or cornered, the Dugite can be quite defensive, with an explosive, open-mouthed, frontal attack. Confrontation should definitely be avoided!

Dugite from South Guildford, Western Australia. Image: Paul Orange

Dugite, melanistic form, Greenmount, Western Australia. Image: Paul Orange

A typical juvenile Dugite, Joondalup, Western Australia. Image: Paul Orange

Dugite from Kabarda–Greenmount, Western Australia. Image: Paul Orange

Northern Brown Snake

Patch-nosed Brown Snake. Image: Ken Griffiths

Black head form of the Gwardar. Image: Paul Orange

Grey head form of the Gwardar. Image: Greg Fyfe

The **Northern Brown Snake**, *Pseudonaja nuchalis*, is confined to the Top End of Australia and is common around Darwin. Predominantly brown, some individuals have a paler head, or faint bands, other have dark flecks or spots along the body. Like all brown snakes, this snake is active during the day and can be more active at night when the wet season occurs. It is quick to flee but will display and bite if seriously provoked. Confrontations can occur in yards, through misidentification. It is attracted to properties for food particularly mice, lizards and other snakes. It may shelter under rubbish, lumber walls, large rocks or dense ground cover.

The **Strap-snouted Brown Snake** *Pseudonaja (nuchalis) aspirdorhyncha* is confined to southern South Australia, north western Victoria and western New South Wales. It has the associated habits of brown snakes, the preference for disturbed regions, predation of mice and lizards. This species overall tends to be a shade of darker brown, but can be light brown. This snake is shy and retiring, when threatened has a lower strike level than other brown snakes preferring to strike low.

The **Western Brown Snake** or **Gwardar,** *Pseudonaja (nuchalis) mengdeni,* is a very alert, nervous and fast-moving snake. There are two forms: one has a beautiful orange reddish body with a black head; the other has a greyish head on a lighter brown body. It is widely distributed and is the main call out for Central Australian communities including Alice Springs and major parts of Western Australia. It commonly forages for rodents, pet birds and lizards around backyards, homesteads and sheds. It shelters under large piles of debris, rock piles, rodent holes, sheets of corrugated iron and also haystacks and old machinery. Quick to flee, it will display and bite if provoked.

Brown snakes are commonly confused with:

ACT	Juvenile brown snakes are often confused with the Little Whip Snake, Mitchell's Short-tailed Snake or the hooded snake. Juvenile banded or ringed brown snakes are often confused with the Rough-scaled Snake or the Eastern Tiger Snake.
NSW	Lowland Copperheads, Spotted Black Snakes (Brown forms), Mulga Snake and Yellow-faced Whip Snake
NT	Mulga Snake, Yellow-faced Whip Snake
QLD	Mulga Snake, Spotted Black Snakes (Brown Forms), Coastal Taipan, Yellow-faced Whip Snake
SA	Mulga Snake, Lowland and Pygmy Copperheads, Yellow–faced Whip Snake and Peninsula Brown Snake
WA	Mulga Snake, Yellow-faced Whip Snake
VIC	Lowland Copperheads, Yellow-faced Whip Snake

Other venomous snakes

The Rough-scaled Snake (60 cm–1 m) is found in the coastal regions of north-eastern Australia from Barrington Tops in the south up to Cairns and Cape Tribulation. It is mostly active at night. It has a light brown to olive-brown body, often with narrow cross-bands. Its belly is cream, olive or yellow, often with dark blotches. It looks similar and occurs in similar habitats to the harmless Keelback. While quick to escape, the Rough-scaled Snake assumes an aggressive stance if cornered that is not typical of smaller snakes. It will strike repeatedly and hiss loudly. Its venom is potent, and a bite can have severe effects. It has been responsible for several fatalities.

Image: Martin Baxter

Potentially dangerously venomous

The Small-eyed Snake is a secretive species, almost completely nocturnal. It is common in Sydney, Brisbane, Townsville and Cairns and much of the eastern coast. It ranges in size from 45–80 cm. Image: Nick Clemann

Potentially dangerously venomous

Stephen's Banded Snake is occasionally seen around properties in its isolated range. It is easily provoked and considered potentially dangerous. It grows from 60 cm to 1 m. Some specimens may be unbanded. Image: Lyall Naylor

Venomous; potentially harmful

The nocturnal Curl Snake has surprisingly strong venom. It grows to about 45 cm and is occasionally seen in yards looking for reptiles, frogs and small mammals.

Venomous; considered harmless

The small Dwarf-crowned Snake is nocturnal. It has a very narrow yellow collar and its belly surface is yellow with thin black bands. It grows to about 45 cm. Image: John Weigel

Venomous; considered harmless

The Golden-crowned Snake (40–70 cm) is active by night. It has a broken golden-brown collar. Its belly is orange with a prominent row of black blotches running down the centre. Image: Stewart McDonald

Venomous; considered harmless

The White-lipped Snake is associated with coastal regions of swamps, creeks and heathland. It grows to about 30 cm and can be seen during daylight hours under debris or basking among vegetation or logs. It usually flees quickly when approached. Image: Nick Clemann

Venomous; considered harmless

The Southern Half-girdled Snake (35 cm) is a burrowing species that feeds on reptile eggs. It is usually unearthed during gardening and is sometimes brought in by cats at night. Image: Paul Orange

Venomous; considered harmless

The Black-bellied Swamp Snake or Marsh Snake (50 cm) is associated with swamps, wetlands, creeks, coastal plains and heathland of northern New South Wales and Queensland. It is active by day. Image: Lyall Naylor

The nocturnal Red-naped Snake (about 40 cm) is easily identified by its colour. Image: Stewart McDonald

The Little Whip Snake is active at night. It grows to about 30 cm.

The Yellow-faced Whipsnake is active by day. It grows to about 65 cm in length.

Image: Ken Griffiths.

The Black Whipsnake is usually about 60 cm in length. It is active by night and day.

Image: Stewart McDonald

Sea snakes

Sea snakes form an intriguing group of front fanged venomous snakes. They are generally found in the warmer waters of northern Australia, but individuals occasionally turn up in southern waters. When strong offshore or cyclonic conditions wash them ashore, they can be a hazard for fisherfolk or bathers.

Sea snakes have a distinctive paddle-shaped tail and often rough skin. They can bite and care is needed if rescuers are handling them. The most likely seen sea snakes are **Stoke's Sea Snake**, *Astrotia stokesii*, **Hardwick Sea Snake**, *Lapemis hardwickii*, and sometimes the **Yellow-bellied Sea Snake**, *Pelamis platurus*, which is highly venomous. It is a highly distinctive species with yellow underneath and blue on top.

All sea snakes are classed as dangerously venomous and care is needed when handling them. Their venom can cause damage and a bite needs to be treated with sea snake antivenom.

The Yellow-bellied Sea Snake grows to between 1 and 2 m in length. This one has been washed ashore near Sydney, New South Wales.

Image: Ken Griffiths.

6 Snakes around your house

Many people spend a large proportion of their time in and around the house, so it's not surprising that around 30–40 per cent of snakebites occur here. While some bites (such as those of the Eastern Brown Snake) may be 'dry bites', all bites should be treated as serious, but medical treatment is such that they are very manageable and fatalities are rare.

Houses situated in dense suburbia are less likely to have slithery visitors, while rural properties and houses close to remnant bushland, parks, national parks or conservation reserves are more likely to have snakes. Snakes may enter properties for a wide range of reasons; however, there is strong evidence that food and shelter are the two most likely factors leading to a snake visit.

A source of food

Food for snakes has never been more abundant than in our yards. Urban environments have become a haven

Baby mice – a bonanza for any foraging snake.

An Eastern Tiger Snake in an aviary, Yarra Valley, Victoria.

A Diamond Python in ambush position, in the rafters of an old shed. Image: John Weigel

for the three food types most likely to attract a snake to you: mammals, lizards and birds. Rodents – primarily introduced rats and mice – are strongly favoured prey for many of the larger snake species.

Mice have made themselves at home across Australia. They can reproduce in large colonies and have extensive tracks or pathways around the yard. These tracks can be scented from hundreds of metres away by foraging snakes.

Snakes are often the number one predator of rodents around the house, but they are also on the lookout for other mammals such as pet rabbits, guineapigs and possums. Brush-tailed Possums and Ring-tailed Possums make up a large part of carpet python diets.

Lizards – especially skinks – play an essential ecological role in the diet of snakes, particularly many of the smaller elapid species, while the juveniles of most snakes initially prey on skinks to get started in life. The abundance of skinks certainly provides foraging snakes something to feed on.

Overgrown gardens and walkways will attract snakes and present a danger to your family.

Birds make up a substantial part of the diet of some species, in particular pythons and the larger elapid species like tiger snakes, the Mulga Snake and the Brown Tree Snake. While pest bird species may be preyed upon, it is far more likely that your pet birds get taken. While lovebirds, budgerigars, cockatiels and lorikeets are most likely prey, even cockatoos, ducks and chickens may be taken by large carpet pythons and the Scrub Python.

Q Do blue-tongued lizards keep snakes away?

A Not necessarily. Although they may keep some smaller snakes away (intimidating them with their size or a threat display), larger species such as brown snakes or copperheads will prey on them. However, they do occupy homesites that may have been used by snakes.

Your garden

The garden not only provides shelter and food, it is also a great source of moisture and water. Many gardens with a north aspect are favoured in spring and winter while the cooler aspects are used in summer. Water features or ponds provide a natural source of water for snakes and a humid environment for sloughing. The pond also attracts frogs and small lizards, making it a good location for snakes to forage in. Frogs may be a food source for some snakes but they appear to be incidental to a snake visit.

In most gardens there are many potential shelter sites for snakes – hollow logs, retaining walls, piles of rocks, plants e.g. fish ferns, *Agapanthus*, ivy, creepers or native grasses. Then there may be sheets of galvanised iron behind the shed, the outdoor shed with its roof space, the firewood, and disused car parts, especially bonnets. There's also the compost heap, a wonderful source of food, heat, and humidity, especially for blind snakes, tiger snakes and, in Brisbane, various species of the Crowned Snake.

Old timber retaining walls are great for snakes.

Some people store a whole lot of 'stuff' in their backyard that provides a refuge for snakes – old roof tiles, rolls of plastic, garden mesh, old tyres, lawn-mowers – the list is quite extensive.

Occasionally the odd spot, gas heaters, gutters, and roof spaces will provide a home for pythons. Large trees (especially *Eucalyptus* species) will have hollows that suit many of the larger pythons, especially Carpet Pythons and Scrub Pythons. Strangely enough letterboxes attract some snakes – particularly the Rough-scaled Snake in Far North Queensland.

Prevention and property maintenance

In order to deter these unwelcome visitors, the house is a good place to start. During hot weather, smaller elapids are forced into buildings to escape the hot ground surface, often squeezing through gaps in windows, doors and walls. The startling truth is that snakes can manoeuvre through gaps only 1 cm or so in width. So start with the doors – a rubber strip along the bottom on both sides will close the gap. Windows should have well-fitted flyscreens with no obvious holes. Open windows, especially in northern tropical areas, are often how various snakes such as pythons or tree snakes can get in at night.

Beware of snakes basking, especially in cooler months. They bask in open areas around the house as well as on paths and tracks in parkland and in the bush.

Fencing can still be a major deterrent for snake visits. Keep it sealed down low. If you are using traditional paling fences, these tend to have gaps at the bottom for water to flow under and eventually rotting sets in. It is important to seal this gap using mesh, shade cloth, fibroboard, plywood or other outdoor material, dug in to a depth of 20 cm and nailed along the fence line – hard and tedious work I admit. This is only a short-term gap measure especially as rabbits and rats sometimes gnaw their way through.

In areas where pythons occur, it is useful to investigate the roof space for their presence. It is important to seal the cavities and holes where rats and possums have been

Many snake visits go unnoticed as the snake passes through, foraging for food or searching for a mate. A homeowner could easily miss seeing this Slatey-grey Snake as it moves across the driveway.

gaining entry. Once the roof is mammal-proofed and sealed, the chance of a snake coming in is greatly reduced.

The space under your house may often provide a temporary shelter site for snakes escaping the heat or when attacked. It can be a case of storing too much timber or other potential refuge material under your house that attracts the snake to shelter. It helps to raise the stored goods off the ground using old crates, wooden boxes etc. in order to create a space of roughly 40–60 cm. This helps to detect any unwanted visitor – a quick flash of the torch will reveal the presence of a snake.

In maintaining your property, remember that most snakebites occur when snakes are trodden on. This can be prevented by having cleared walkways. Ensure that the footpaths to the door and car are free from overgrown vegetation. Shrubs, ground covers and large tussock grasses can grow over the path. These need to be trimmed

Ponds attract frogs and snakes. Keeping your pond clear of growth may help to deter snakes.

or pruned to ensure that a snake is not hidden from the view of a person walking along the path. The path is a wonderful basking spot for snakes; nocturnal snakes find it a great place to maintain their temperature.

Your garden is a great place for the snake to feel secure, feed, slough, and rest. Garden maintenance is therefore critical in order to remove the welcome mat for snakes! On arriving at a property, most experienced snake catchers can decide within minutes what the snake is doing, which species it is likely to be and possibly where it is. Gardeners pride themselves on how the garden is maintained – the plants blend in with the cascading waterfalls, the retaining wall obscured by climbers, a solid wall of ivy all along the fence. In this situation there is a huge challenge. Gardeners rightly love their garden, so where do we draw a line for snakes and plants? If you have a new house and the garden is not yet established, we can do something. Begin by ensuring that all plants that are ground covering are up the back. Any plants near the door, both front and back, should be species that can be pruned, shaped or kept from the surface. Small shrubs are fine but prune the base to keep them open. Remember most dangerous species are terrestrial. Keep large shrubs and trees away from the house, trim them off the roof and prune back as far as possible.

Frogs such as this Green Tree Frog are prey for snakes.

Long grass is attractive to snakes. Why? Because they feel secure from predators as they work their way along the foraging trail. They dislike intensely being exposed in the open. Quite often a snake will follow a scent trail left by mice that are using the grass for the same reason at night – to avoid being picked up by owls. Keep your grass short and pay particular attention to the fence lines. Use a whipper-snipper to prevent a hidden trail forming along the fence.

The garden shed is often the place where we store all those goods that eventually become just a haphazard pile inside this outbuilding. It's true that snakes frequent sheds mostly to escape detection or when foraging. Keep it

Rural and large vacant lots regularly need a slash both for fire prevention and for snake reduction.

Keep areas around sheds and outhouses clear.

Stack iron sheets off the ground with bricks or small boxes.

simple in the shed – store any feed inside sealed drums. Use racks to keep food off the ground.

There are several important aspects of snake prevention techniques. First, in rural and bushland properties, snake prevention is very similar to fire prevention. The removal of dry timber and having cleared regions also facilitate a safer environment for children and visitors.

You have worked hard, keeping the yard unfriendly but you can still get a visit. Snakes will often take a chance if the reward is greater than the risk. So let's remove the rewards, where possible.

Rodent control is the first and primary concern, for the residence or farm. Mice can exist in plague proportions in some years. We need to prevent any populations from living in the house especially, but pay attention to the shed, compost and attic as well as under the house. There are several brands of rodent bait: follow the instructions and remember to place the bait in areas where pets and children cannot get access. Bait regularly in spring, summer and during winter. For serious rodent control, contact your local pest controller.

Pest birds can be a little harder to control. Avoid bird-feeding stations, which inevitably attract both birds and mice. Remove any nests along the roof, gutters and bordering trees. Ensure that they do not belong to native birds as they are protected.

Q Will a saucer of milk attract snakes?

A No! Snakes do not drink milk!

How snakey are you?

Not snakey
You have no parks, paddocks, undeveloped land or waterways within 2 km; you have a very tidy yard, and are completely surrounded by houses.

Snakish
You have a small amount of vacant land nearby, or some isolated parks with ponds or lakes, but you are predominantly surrounded by houses.

Snakey
Your property is within 1000 m of large areas of vacant land, parks, bushland or a waterway; your yard is landscaped with overgrown gardens; you have ponds and clutter from debris and storage; you have pest birds and rodents in your property; your neighbours complain of snakes.

Very snakey
Your property backs directly onto a national park, acres of bushland or a heavily vegetated waterway; you have an overgrown garden or ponds, and clutter from debris and storage. You have pest birds and rodents in the property; your neighbours complain of snakes, or you have a large or hobby style farm, with rodents, shed clutter and excessively overgrown gardens.

A well manicured and mown lawn is a very effective snake prevention technique.

7 Living with lizards

Australia has a wonderful and diverse range of lizards – we have more than 600 species. They exist in nearly all habitats from alpine regions to the deserts; we have lizards throughout our forests, heathlands, grasslands, urban habitats and waterways.

Lizards have well-developed eyesight; they also have ear openings. Most of them have legs, and some species, especially skinks, geckos and legless lizards can shed their tails in defence. In most cases lizards rarely affect house owners, aside from the shock of seeing a blue tongue hiss or move. However, some lizards, especially monitor lizards, can cause annoyance when they raid chicken pens, forage in the roof of a house and become a persistent visitor. Lizards usually pose very little threat to us although some people worry for their pets and choose to have lizards removed. This chapter looks at the lizard families and the most common offenders around

Yellow Spotted Monitors are common in rural outback properties from north-western Australia to Queensland.

Image: Brad Maryan

Widespread across Australia, the Sand Goanna or Gould's Goanna is also commonly seen around properties.

domestic situations.

Monitor lizards (Goannas)

This spectacular group of lizards gets its name as a corrupted version of 'Iguana' given by early settlers. The name goanna has stuck ever since. They vary greatly from the small Short-tailed Pygmy Goanna at around 25 cm to the world's second largest lizard the **Perentie**, *Varanus giganteus,* at 2.5 m in length. Goannas provided indigenous Australians with good 'tucker' – they found the Perentie particularly tasty.

Monitor lizards are carnivorous. They have very good eyesight which, combined with their athletic bodies, enables them to run down fast-moving lizards and mammals. They have a forked tongue, similar to a snake, and a great sense of smell which allows them to locate burrowing animals so they can be dug out. They will dig up frogs, centipedes and also are quite good at getting rabbits. They will also tackle snakes including venomous species. It has never been shown that they are immune

These Lace Monitors are feeding on a dead wallaby. Image: John Weigel

to snake venom – it is more likely that their tough sandpaper-like skin acts as a tough barrier that snake fangs cannot penetrate. Some larger goannas are fond of roadkill which offers a substantial feed for a small output of energy. This of course makes them prone to being killed by road traffic.

It has been recently shown that monitor lizards, along with other so-called harmless snakes actually have very primitive venom glands. While their venom is not in the same class as that of elapid snakes, there is some evidence that it can cause a very mild disturbance to blood. Monitor lizards – especially those that feed on carrion – also have some very harmful bacteria in their mouth which makes a bite from them painful with potential medical complications. Monitors also have very sharp claws that can also cause injury.

Large monitors have quite an appetite. They forage across a wide area, travelling up to several kilometres in search of food. Your backyard may offer a quick and easy meal. Monitors may raid chicken pens, aviaries, forage through rubbish bins, compost heaps and eat dead lambs, but – despite a common rural belief – have never been seen to kill them. A monitor will also climb a tree to prey on bird nests and eat the nestlings or eggs.

The **Lace Monitor**, *Varanus varius*, occurs along the eastern seaboard, mostly associated with woodlands. It is semi-arboreal and will spend large amounts of time in trees, basking or foraging. It can be a problem lizard for farmers, chicken and duck breeders, as it may frequent yards that back onto large tracts of remnant bushland. The Lace Monitor tolerates humans well, but may turn and defend itself if chased. Sometimes it will become a nuisance at camp grounds, raiding rubbish bins or approaching tables when food is being prepared. The

Q Are Australian lizards venomous?

A The simple answer is mostly 'no', but monitor lizards have venom that can cause shock, pain (hyperalgesia), coagulopathy, and tissue destruction.

Image: Lyall Naylor

feeding of monitors at campgrounds should be strongly discouraged.

The **Black-headed Monitor**, *Varanus tristis*, is a medium-sized semi-arboreal monitor that frequents woodlands, and is widely distributed across Australia. It is found in yards in Perth and Alice Springs, and also on rural or outback properties. Often described as: 'scratching around in the roof', it will often reside in the roof space when foraging or overwintering. Typically shy, it can be seen basking near trees, on rooftops or when foraging on the ground. It is quick to escape into the tree or roof if disturbed!

A Lace Monitor trapped inside a wire pen is enough to raise the ire of any poultry farmer. All reptiles are protected and can not be harmed or moved.

Some goanna species frequent picnic areas and yards to forage for food scraps. They may even take food from people who are silly enough to offer it. Wildlife – especially goannas – should never be fed, as this carries the risk of injury to you and others.

Goannas should not be approached or captured if in the yard. Patience will see them off after a day or two. However, it is wise to monitor-proof your chook pen using heavy gauge mesh. Naughty lizards can be hosed away quite easily.

The Lace Monitor can become a nuisance at camp grounds in the eastern states.

Black-headed Monitor.

Image: Brian Bush

Confrontations between dogs and monitors occur readily. Monitors have an impressive threat display which, if ignored, may lead to a tail thrash which is very strong and has certainly been known to seriously injure dogs. If your pet is bitten by a monitor, it should be treated by a vet. If a person receives a bite from a monitor, it is essential to treat the bite using a strong antiseptic and have a doctor assess it. Antibiotics may be necessary to control the subsequent bacterial infection. It is not true that goanna bites flare up each year. However, they can be difficult to heal if not properly treated and, even if treated, may heal slowly.

Snails are a preferred food item for blue-tongue lizards.

Skinks

Skinks form Australia's largest lizard group, with over 390 species, including some of the world's largest species – the Land Mullet and Eastern Blue-tongue Lizard. Skinks occupy all niche types and can be found in all habitats except for the most inhospitable. They are often a prime food source for small or juvenile snakes. They rarely present problems in urban environments merely being cheeky in the vegetable or strawberry patch. Blue tongues and Shingleback lizards thrive on rotting vegetation and especially the introduced European Snail. Small skinks scurry through leaf litter, in rocky outcrops or in and out of bark or tree hollows.

Most skinks are quite small and just about every garden in Australia has them. Mostly they are insectivorous with larger species tending to eat more plant material. They are drawn to gardens with plenty of cover where they forage for invertebrates among the leaf litter. These bright, friendly fellows are of no consequence to people in yards. Sometimes a domestic cat will prey on them and bring them into the house. They also act as essential prey for small snakes and the hatchlings of larger snake species. However, the larger skinks can be mistaken for snakes – often the sight

A blue-tongue lizard hiding in dense grass is easily mistaken for a snake. Image: Stewart McDonald

The Eastern Blue-tongue Lizard is one of the world's largest members of the skink family, Scincidae.

of something big and banded looking in the grass is enough for the homeowner to call for help.

The most widespread and well-known lizard is arguably the **Eastern Blue-tongue Lizard,** *Tiliqua scincoides*. We have been accustomed to seeing this lizard from the early settler days and huge numbers are now adapted to urban life.

Western Australia has the **Western Blue-tongue Lizard,** *Tiliqua occipitalis*, which is similar in behaviour to its eastern cousin.

The Eastern Blue-tongued Lizard can be a ready companion in the yard basking especially in spring months, quietly roaming looking for areas containing its favourite food – the introduced snail. While it also will eat fungi and rotting vegetation, it also has acquired some taste for strawberries, as any farmer will tell you. Around late summer/early autumn you may notice a surge in numbers as baby lizards appear. These typically disperse over a month. Your yard can only support a small number of lizards permanently. Lazing with blue-tongues means watch out when mowing the lawn, reversing the car out on the concrete driveway especially in spring and when baiting snails.

Blotched Blue-tongue Lizard.

The **Blotched Blue-tongue Lizard**, *Tiliqua nigrolutea*, is common in NSW, Victoria and Tasmania and its offshore islands including Flinders Island. This is a large patterned skink that also displays its vivid cobalt blue tongue when threatened. It can be found at high elevations up 1000 m and inhabits the cooler climatic regions including areas that have snow. It is live bearing with up to eight young born free and no maternal care is given. This lizard is commonly seen in areas around properties especially in dense gardens and retaining walls.

The **Shingleback,** *Tiliqua rugosa*, is a semi-arid specialist that favours farmyards and bush blocks in south-eastern Australia as well as the south-west, and around Perth.

The Shingleback has many other common names. It is called the Bobtail in Western Australia, the Sleepy Lizard in South Australia, the Boggi in western New South Wales and the Stumpytail in Victoria. This wonderful lizard has some unique aspects. It is one of the few known lizards

The Northern Blue-tongue Lizard, a much larger robust lizard, is common in yards around Darwin and much of northern Australia.

Common across Australia, Western Blue-tongue lizards are seen in rural and outback properties feeding on vegetation and snails. Image: Lyall Naylor

The Shingleback has many other common names: Boggi, Stumpy-tailed Lizard, Sleepy Lizard and Pine Cone Lizard.

to be monogamous – it remains paired with the same partner for a number of years. Shinglebacks can recognise their offspring which, when born, remain attached to them for a few weeks. They are omnivorous, yet will take on some insects or carrion when the opportunity arises. They wander around properties, shelter under galvanised iron or, more likely, under small ground shrubs. Their loudly hissing threat display with an open mouth and tongue protruding is an impressive sight to see. However, once accustomed to your presence, they will go about their business with no ill effects to you or your family.

Skinks are both egg layers and live bearers with most large species live bearing, including members of *Tiliqua*.

The **Pink-tongued Skink,** *Cyclodomorphus gerrardii*, is a graceful skink, with a prehensile tail and long claws that enable it to climb and forage for its favourite food – snails. It is strikingly marked and grows to 30 cm. Because of its thin body, it is often mistaken for a snake especially in the dimly lit areas of wet forest where it often occurs.

Pink-tongued Skink.

Image: Stewart McDonald

Dragons

The family Agamidae includes the iconic Frilled Lizard, the well-known Bearded Dragon (perhaps the most kept pet lizard in the world) and the water dragons.

Dragons are usually insectivorous, although the larger species tend to be omnivorous. The Bearded Dragon loves yellow flowers, insects and grasses, while the Frilled Lizard eats mostly invertebrates.

All dragons lay eggs which usually hatch in late summer. Dragons also are most prolific in spring when they first emerge from winter. They feed heavily and regularly bask, as well as becoming reproductive.

When threatened, dragons rely on speed to flee up trees, into logs, stumps or down holes. Some dragons have a threat display, which consists of an open mouth and hissing. Some lizards inflate their body and/or display a frill or large region of gular commonly referred to as a

The iconic Frilled Lizard.

beard! Dragons will bite if handled and careful attention should be given to bites from large lizards.

The **Frilled Lizard**, *Chlamydosaurus kingii*, 'We like our dragons frilled not grilled' is a famous slogan for bushfire prevention. The Frilled Lizard is a spectacular lizard that is under some pressure from Cane Toads. It may feed on metamorphling (baby) Cane Toads, which are active during the day and which resemble a small beetle to this lizard. Often seen incidentally around properties, Frilled Lizards rarely present a problem.

The **Eastern Water Dragon**, *Physignathus lesueurii lesueurii*, is a very urban species, common in Sydney and Brisbane. It is usually associated with waterways like creeks, rivers and lakes. This lizard's habit of diving into the water when spooked usually means it is heard but not seen. Quick to become unafraid of people whose properties provide a suitable habitat, these dragons will colonise areas and become tame where there are artificial waterways such as ponds and fountains.

The Eastern Water Dragon is common in urban gardens close to waterways.

The Central Bearded Dragon, like many reptiles, enjoys basking on the road.

The Eastern Bearded Dragon is fond of perching on stumps or fence posts.

The **Bearded Dragon**, *Pogona barbata*, is common in many parts of Australia and is one of the world's most popular exotic pets. It occurs mostly in woodlands, grassland, semi arid heathland and coastal heath. Largely associated with fallen branches, it has also adapted to wood fence lines and often can be seen perched on stumps or fence posts. It is common on farms and bush blocks. This lizard is largely insectivorous when young and omnivorous when adult.

Legless lizards

The legless lizards are oftern mistaken for worms or snakes. They belong to the family Pygopodidae. Some legless lizards are thin and small as a worm, but without the rugged shiny scales of blind snakes, they are clearly a different species. The larger legless lizards have evolved with some mimicry and look superficially similar to juvenile venomous snakes with adapted defence postures to those of the snakes!

Legless lizards are encountered only occasionally – you are more likely to come across a juvenile venomous snake. Legless lizards have an ear opening just back from the eye, and a fleshy tongue which they use to lick clean the surface of their eyes. They also have the remnant of legs in the form of hind flaps on their sides close to the cloaca. They move in a distinctively lizard-like fashion but, to a casual observer, are still mistaken for a snake. Unfortunately, many are killed because they are so snake-like.

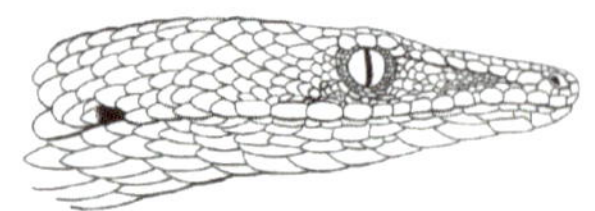

Ear opening of Burton's Snake Lizard. Illustration: Rachel Hammond

Legless lizards are insectivorous except for **Burton's Snake Lizard,** *Lialis burtonis*, which preys on other lizards. The largest legless lizard, it is a very distinctive lizard with a long snout, sometimes with stripes. It often may be seen active at night moving through the garden or along roads and paths. It can also be found during the day when lifting tin, rocks, logs or when doing garden maintenance of tussock grasses.

The most commonly encountered legless lizard is Burton's Snake Lizard, which grows to about 40 cm in length. Image: John Weigel

Olive Legless Lizard.

The **Olive Legless Lizard (Patternless Delma)**, *Delma inornata*, is a temperate grassland species, replaced in mallee by the similar looking *D. butleri*. *Delma molleri* is still pretty common in Adelaide suburbs. Melburnians and Canberrans live alongside the endangered *D. impar*. In Perth they have *D. fraseri* and *D. grayii*.

Geckos

There is a wide range of gecko species occurring in many habitat types, foraging on trees, sheltering in rocks or caves, under the bark of trees and also in houses. Some species have become urbanised and may be found in all capital cities except for Hobart. We also have two intruders from overseas – the Asian House Gecko and the Mourning Gecko. The Asian House Gecko is vocal at night with its 'chuk chuk' sounds. It is territorial and quite aggressive, and will attack smaller local species. They are very strong predators and can eat spiders and cockroaches and other insects.

The Asian House Gecko is common in northern Australian residential regions. Image: Lyall Naylor

Marbled Gecko.

The **Marbled Gecko**, *Christinus marmoratus,* is the southernmost occurring gecko common in Melbourne and throughout Victoria into New South Wales and South Australia. While usually living under the exfoliating bark of large trees, it adapts readily to urban living.

Q Do geckos have suction pads on their feet?

A Actually geckos have very fine adhesive hairs which allow them to cling to smooth surfaces such as walls or glass and climb other surfaces when chasing insects! Not all geckos have this ability – some species have claws and are more suited to living on the ground.

Image: Stewart MacDonald

8 Living with crocodiles

It seems ironic that our oldest living reptiles, with origins dating back millions of years, are treated with such little awareness and respect. Australia has two crocodile species – the Freshwater (or Johnston's) Crocodile and the Saltwater (or Estuarine) Crocodile. The Freshwater Crocodile is almost exclusively found in fresh water but the Saltwater Crocodile is typically found in both. It has a larger movement pattern, home range and territorial region.

The **Freshwater Crocodile**, *Crocodylus johnstoni*, is the smaller of the two species, with an average length of about 2 m, although some specimens can grow to 3 m. It inhabits inland freshwater creeks, rivers and billabongs, feeding mainly on fish but also insects, spiders, turtles, small reptiles, and water rats. Reptile catchers in the Northern Territory are sometimes called to remove small Freshwater Crocodiles from pools and spas.

Freshwater Crocodile.

Image: Stewart MacDonald

The **Saltwater Crocodile**, *Crocodylus porosus*, is the main threat to people, livestock and domestic pets. This crocodile inhabits open saltwater, bays, mudflats, estuaries, creeks and rivers inland and freshwater lagoons and billabongs. It will eat crabs, fish, birds, other reptiles and mammals, including pigs and dogs. With an average length of about 4 m, large individuals may grow up to 5.5 m.

Saltwater Crocodiles are territorial – especially the males. Females will defend and protect nesting sites from other crocodiles and predators e.g. pigs, goannas and people. The larger males will establish a home range, which they vigorously defend against other crocodiles. Males will investigate strange shapes – such as a canoe moving through their range.

Some crocodiles exhibit interesting behaviour. One Northern Territory crocodile named 'Sweetheart' was estimated to be 50 years old, weighed 750 kg and was more than 5 m long. He persistently attacked aluminum

Saltwater Crocodiles, particularly large individuals, are the main threat to people, livestock and domestic pets. This specimen is from Bloomfield in Queensland.

Image: Lyall Naylor

Rangers in Western Australia, Northern Territory and Queensland are trained to remove 'nuisance' crocodiles.
Image: Chris Pederby

boats that entered his domain. He was adept at attacking propellers of outboard motors, resulting in boats being overturned. He was finally caught in July 1979 and is now preserved in the Northern Territory Museum and Art Gallery in Fannie Bay, Darwin.

Female crocodiles will harbour and protect their offspring. They reproduce in the wet season, with the female crocodile laying around 50 eggs at a time. Female Saltwater Crocodiles scratch metre-high nests from vegetative matter such as grass, bark and leaves. The area around the nest must offer seclusion, protection from flooding, a basking spot and a quick path to the water. She will stay with the nest, defending it where necessary.

Due to the territorial behaviour of the males, juveniles are forced to move out of their original home range and look for a new territory. If they do not leave, they run the risk of being maimed or killed by the adult males. Only about 1 per cent will survive to maturity – 17 years for males and around 12 years for females.

Reptile catchers are sometimes called to remove small Freshwater Crocodiles from pools and spas.
Image: Chris Pederby

Q Is the sex of baby crocodiles determined by nest temperature?

A Yes, below 31°C the hatchlings will be female, those at 32°C will be male, and hatchlings at 33°C and above will be female. This system ensures that the sex that needs to grow biggest (males) is hatched from eggs at the optimum temperature (32° in this case).

Q How do crocodiles communicate?

A Crocodilians communicate with each other with sounds that they make by forcing air through a voice box in the throat. Adults make loud low roars to each other and may hiss and growl (salties are quiet relative to other species). When a male and a female mate, they often purr softly .The young call (in squeaks) to the adults when they are in danger and make lots of noise while they are being fed.

In the warmer months of the Top End wet season, crocodiles enjoy the warm water and only need to bask infrequently. The flooding of rivers and billabongs and local rivers can also allow Saltwater Crocodiles to end up in strange and unusual places. The local rangers and reptile catchers remove around 10–20 crocodiles in these circumstances annually. Northern Territory Parks and Wildlife officers capture more than 200 crocodiles ranging from 2.5 to 4 m in length each year from Darwin Harbour.

In autumn, the air cools slightly and the crocodiles emerge on banks to bask for extra warmth. During winter months, June to August, they regularly bask on river banks for long periods and maintain low energy outputs. The water is very cool and digestion is kept low. Spring brings crocodiles into heavier feeding, males engage in combat and strong territory disputes are common.

Crocodiles are usually wary of people and areas with high human density. However, they can become a 'nuisance' animal when attracted to areas such as boat ramps where fishermen often clean their catches. Fishing charters that clean their catch and feed crocodiles to entertain their clients, or tour operators who feed wild crocodiles, may inadvertently be encouraging these animals to become too familiar with us.

Many crocodile attacks occur from November to March during the wet season. It is not only larger individuals, but crocodiles only 2 m or so in length can be involved. In some cases, crocodiles will be attracted to and attack fish that have been recently caught on fishing lines. Crocodiles will go after dogs as well as other animals, including livestock, that go near the water's edge.

Northern Territory Crocodile warning signs should never be ignored. Image: Chris Pederby

Warning signs are placed in high risk areas and must always be obeyed. Crocodiles can become familiar with your patterns of activity. For example, do not perform the same routine at campsites, such as getting water from the water's edge. Saltwater Crocodiles can swim under water at 30 km/h without a ripple on the surface and then burst out and, over a short distance, can outrun a horse. If a prey puts up too much resistance they will do the 'death roll' to get it off its feet.

The crocodile is a top-order predator whose finely tuned senses have evolved from millions of years of nature's lessons. We need to take the presence of crocodiles into account when we are in their habitats. These magnificent animals should not be penalised for taking people as food when we often gift-wrap ourselves as such.

Key points for crocodile safety

- Do not attract or encourage crocodiles by cleaning fish near the water.
- Pay attention to crocodile warning signs.
- Avoid a routine visit to the water's edge when fishing or getting camping water.
- Tour operators should not feed crocodiles for entertainment.
- Avoid having dogs near the water's edge.
- Teach your children to be on the lookout for crocodiles.
- Report any sighting of a crocodile to the local CrocWatch agency.
- Be especially wary of waterholes after big rains where crocodiles can be washed into new locations.

Report crocodile sightings to the EPA Hotline 1300 130 372.
In the case of a crocodile attack, telephone 000.

9 Living with Cane Toads

The **Cane Toad,** *Bufo marinus*, is the only true member of the toad family in Australia. It was introduced into Edmonton, Queensland, in 1935, in an attempt to control the Greyback Cane Beetle, *Dermolepida albohirtum*. However, the ability of these animals to reach a beetle that lived in the higher stalks of sugar cane was overestimated, and the Cane Toad turned out to be totally unsuitable as a control agent.

The Cane Toad rather quickly moved out of the cane fields into the more lush surrounding habitats of Far North Queensland, causing devastation to many native species – including frog-eating snakes. Because of the toad's unique toxins, almost anything that eats it dies rapidly from heart failure. The Cane Toad has since invaded New South Wales, the Northern Teritory, and has moved into Western Australia, including the Kimberley region.

Adult Cane Toad foraging at night in Western Australia.
Image: Ken Griffiths

Female Cane Toad. Image: Kimberley Toadbusters Inc.

Freshwater Crocodile with a toxic Cane Toad. Image: Mike Lentic

The Cane Toad is a voracious feeder – consuming insects, reptiles, other frogs, small birds (nestlings or eggs), sometimes small mammals and even roadkill. It has made a home in the World Heritage Kakadu National Park, where its effect on native frogs, the Rainbow Bee-eaters, the Northern Quolls, Johnston's Crocodiles, monitor lizards, Death Adders, Mulga Snakes and Frill-necked Lizards has been simply devastating.

However, no native animal species has yet been made extinct by the Cane Toad, and no human fatalities have

Cane Toad facts

- Cane Toads need to eat up to 200 prey items a night.
- Females are much larger, usually around 12–15 cm.
- Females can lay 20 000–50 000 eggs.
- They secrete a toxin called bufotoxin from glands on the side of the head.
- All forms of the toad are poisonous, the eggs, tadpoles, metamorphlings and adult toads.

Cane Toad myths

- They can spit or fire their venom.
- They poison waterways.
- Nothing can eat them.
- You can safely use them as hallucinogens.
- It's OK to be cruel to them as they are a pest.

The Northern Barred Frog is often mistakenly killed in Far North Queensland.

The Pobblebonk or 'Banjo' Frog is commonly mistaken for the Cane Toad in south-eastern Australia.

been reported. However, pets have been heavily affected in some areas, especially dogs, that seem to learn to mouth toads in order to get a hallucinogenic reaction.

If you live in a 'no toad' area or outside its known range and you find what you believe is a Cane Toad, it is important to contact your state conservation body. If you live in 'toad' areas, you will need to take steps. First correctly identify the frog species, as there are several Australian species that are frequently misidentified and subsequently killed. Learn the call of the Cane Toad, observe its eggs and what its tadpoles look like. The Cane Toad can be confused with some native frogs including water-holding frogs (*Cyclorana* species), barred frogs (*Mixophyes* species) and burrowing species of *Limnodynastes*, especially the Banjo Frog (or Pobblebonk), *Limnodynastes dumerili*. However, these native frogs lack the distinctive parotid glands, warty backs and distinctive toad hop.

If you find a Cane Toad on your property, first bring your pets inside. Unfortunately, domestic pets (especially dogs) learn to mouth or lick toads to receive hallucinogenic reactions. The bufotoxin is absorbed directly from the mouth into the blood stream and there is a rapid development of symptoms. Your pet may drool or shake its head. It may tremble and shake and appear

This is a yearling Cane Toad. As it matures, it will lose its patterning.

Q Can any Australian native animals eat toads?

A Cane Toads have been partially or fully eaten by Crows, White-faced Heron, kites, Bush Stone-Curlew, Tawny Frogmouth, Water Rat, White-tailed Rat, wolf spiders, freshwater crayfish and the Saltwater Crocodile. Keelback Snakes also eat small amounts of toads.

Q Is there any way to stop Cane Toads?

A At present, no! Research has been done on pheromones, genetics, poisons, pathogenic bacteria and fungi, nematodes, and tongue worms that stunt the toad's growth. Work is still needed to make sure that native frogs do not become infected. CSIRO researchers have developed a Bohle iridovirus that would stop toads from being able to produce eggs, potentially capable of eventually wiping out the population.

to lack coordination. There may be severe irritation to its eyes, or temporary visual disturbances. It may have difficulty breathing and experience convulsions, and end up in a coma with rapid progression to death.

You should flush your pet's mouth and face with lots of running water. Tilt the animal's head down so that you do not cause your pet to choke. Wash the eyes out well. See your veterinarian urgently.

Protecting your property

To keep toads out of your property, you should seal fence lines with mesh or shade cloth with minimum gaps of 25 mm. Usually a height of 60 cm is necessary to keep the toads out. You can also place 'gutter guard' around ponds to exclude Cane Toads but allow smaller native frogs through. You should remove any Cane Toad eggs from the pond. These are usually string-like black eggs in jelly.

Cane Toad metamorphlings are toxic to wildlife and pose a significant threat to daytime species such as the Frill-necked Lizard.

In the Northern Territory and the Kimberley region, Western Australia, there are active community groups, which actively search areas and collect toads. The idea of 'toadbusting' is that if everyone contributed and

Cane Toad tadpoles. Image: Stewart McDonald

Like all stages of the Cane Toad life cycle, metamorphlings are toxic to wildlife.

Image: Kimberley Toadbusters Inc.

assisted with collecting toads, their impact, breeding and movement would be significantly affected. Invest in a 'toadbuster' style trap to harvest local breeding adults.

One toad caught in the Northern Territory, dubbed 'Toadzilla' by the media, was 205 mm (8") in length and weighed nearly 1 kg.

Euthanasia and disposal

Although they are a pest, Cane Toads are a living organism and cruelty is cruelty. They should not be tortured or maimed for fun. Euthanasia should be done in a manner that's as quick, efficient and painless as possible, given your circumstances. A commercially produced aerosol spray, HopStop®, has recently been approved to control Cane Toads in backyards and other domestic settings.

In larger scale operations, such as those of 'toadbusting' groups, the use of CO_2 is regarded as humane for the euthanasia of Cane Toads. There are also several methods of dealing with small numbers and metamorphlings, such as spraying them with Dettol® or a similar product. However, some states may be against this method and it is advisable to contact your relevant state department to get further information.

Cane Toads should be handled with disposable gloves.

Image: Kimberley Toadbusters Inc.

The FrogWatch Cane Toad trapping mechanism utilises a gate with clear plastic fingers that allow the toads to see into the trap and enter easily. Once inside the trap they cannot get out again.

Image: Graeme Sawyer

If toads do not bother you, it still remains important to not feed them or have food available to them, such as excess dog food in bowls. Clean out ponds with eggs or tadpoles of toads if you are familiar with the identification of such. Dispose of them wisely, so inadvertent ingestion by wildlife cannot occur.

It is important to assist in planned toadbusting operations by controlling as many as you can. It is usually recommended that you trap toads two nights a week. Metamorphlings appear to be vulnerable to environmental and moisture at this time. Adults are very hardy, with animals surviving exposure to temperatures from 4°C through to 40°C.

First Aid

In some cases people can be affected by toxins either through accidental ingestion or when secretions have been squirted. For more information on Cane Toad poisoning, contact the Poisons Information Line on 13 11 26 anywhere in Australia, 24 hours a day, seven days a week.

10 Handling a snake visit

You're going outside – perhaps to the garden shed or to put the clothes on the line. Suddenly something catches the corner of your eye. It's coiled in the fish fern plant … it's a … SNAKE!

Your brain reels at the sight of the intruder as you travel with the speed of light and the accuracy of a cruise missile back into the house.

This is often the scenario a snake catcher finds when called to the rescue. A snake, not moving and probably asleep in the sun, has provoked this alarmed reaction in an adult person!

Having the snake removed by an expert catcher will give you peace of mind in the short term. A catcher usually has the best chance of getting the snake – especially with a bit of help from you. Take some time

It's a snake!

Illustration: Jay Harley

A snake outside

- Always keep an eye on the snake.
- Even if the snake moves, follow it.
- Often a distance of around 3–5 m is fine with snakes.
- Place watchers on as many aspects as possible.
- Call a catcher and get an estimated time of arrival.
- Watch where the snake disappears to.
- Observe any details of its movements, colour, shape and behaviour.
- Never ever try to kill a snake.
- Use prevention methods to force the snake away.
- If a snake catcher is coming; do not provoke or disturb the snake.

to record its behaviour, movement and the general area around the snake i.e. rock wall, creepers. If the snake is right next to the fence basking it may quickly go back under, never to be seen again. Snakes could be foraging and moving about following a mouse trail or looking for nestling birds in bushes. There are certain behaviours that can occur in residential areas, e.g. foraging, basking, moving or tree climbing. This will help the catcher know what the snake may be doing.

A snake catcher can advise you of what you need to do to snake-proof your property in order to prevent further snake visits.

A garden hose is one of the best snake-discouraging tools in your yard. Forget the spade or shovel – leave it in the shed! Obviously you need to exercise care when confronting a snake. The hose allows you to keep a safe distance from the snake. Move slowly, turn the hose on, create a firm jet (if possible get up on a table or chair), work the jet of water onto the snake, hosing in the direction you would like it to go – back under the fence into the bush. The shock of the water will invariably make

Even after all the good work in cleaning up your property, you may still find a snake basking in full view in the sunshine. However, this may mean an easy job for the snake catcher.

it flee, although not always where you want it to go! The essential lesson here is that the snake will not feel comfortable on your property. If it appears again, do the same thing. It will learn it's not a safe haven and move on. This technique is good on farms or large blocks. In smaller, more confined spaces it is less effective.

If a snake keeps using a particular hole, then seal the hole after the snake has left or use some fly spray around the entrance in order to leave a strong poisonous residue that snakes really do not like. This is a temporary measure as the spray doesn't last very long. There are no effective repellents for snakes and I probably would not recommend one.

A snake in the house is usually a more difficult situation to deal with. You will most likely need the help of a snake catcher as soon as possible. Try to keep an eye on the snake so you can report its whereabouts to the catcher. The lack of any idea where the snake may have disappeared to

A snake in the house!

- Confine the snake to a room.
- Close all the doors, and windows where possible.
- Place towels or clothes or blankets under the door gap.
- Maintain an eye on the snake from a elevated position or through the window. Be patient.
- Call a professional snake catcher to help.

remains the most upsetting aspect of a snake catcher's visit.

In many cases, a snake in the house is quite catchable if the owner has a vague idea of where it went. I have in years gone by caught snakes in all rooms of the house, behind fridges, washing machines, under couches, under beds, in boxes, upstairs, in a spa bath, around toilets and even inside a stereo speaker housing!

Snakes often find their way into the kitchen in search of resident mice or rats.

Q Is it true that if baby snakes are around, the mother snake will also be there?

A It is rare, except with pythons, to find adult snakes with young snakes. Most juvenile snakes often hatch from eggs and disperse quickly. Live-bearing snakes are born and then are abandoned by the mother snake to fend for themselves.

Q Is it true that many snakes seen once are never seen again?

A Yes, most snakes either are passing through or, having been confronted, get a fright and take off. It is unusual for snakes to persist around the house for long periods, except for pythons in the roof or small snakes in the compost heap.

What if no catcher can come?

To encourage a snake to exit, close all the doors along the corridor, open both front and back doors, creating an escape route out of the house. If the snake is hiding behind a box, slowly pull the box away with a long handled instrument like a broom. The snake should start to track its way out; usually the sight of a lighted doorway encourages them to exit the house.

If the snake is sheltering under a concrete slab or paving stones, wait until the snake exits and spray the entrance with flyspray or seal the gap so the snake cannot use it. If the thought of sealing a snake into a hole appeals to you remember that you may force him into a less preferred location like your house.

A snake in the roof can be more difficult to deal with, regardless of whether it's a python, tree snake or a tiger snake. In some parts of Australia, pythons will use the roof space to overwinter or spend the dry season in a warm secluded place. Experts are usually essential for rescuing snakes in dangerous or awkward spaces. Pythons will exit usually to forage or especially during humid nights. If you can see the snake has left, seal up all the gaps around the house that the snake is using to gain entry. Once you have done that, check the roof the following day to see if it has come back.

A Black-headed Python seeking moisture? Amusing, but highly unusual. Only in the Northern Territory, right? Image: Chris Pederby

The author wrestles with a 2.5-m Scrub Python in the cramped roof space of a sugar-cane mill in Far North Queensland.

Finding help in your area

Each state has an agency that oversees a list of snake catchers and maintains a licensing system for those that wish to do so commercially. Most of them will charge a fee for their services. 'Snakeline' is an around-the-clock hotline that is run by Australian herpetologists and experienced emergency phone operators. To find a snake catcher, you can also try searching on the internet under 'snake catching' or 'snake catcher', together with the name of your nearest town or city. In an emergency, contact your local police station, call 000, or try a local or state conservation department. Sometimes zoo-keepers or local park rangers who handle reptiles will remove local 'nuisance' snakes for free.

Living with snakes outdoors

Snakebite in the bush is rare, especially when you consider the frequency of other accidents associated with the outdoors. If you belong to a club or society that regularly seeks outdoor adventures, you should consider getting a snake demonstrator in for your group. Not only will it be entertaining but it will also promote your understanding of our reptile fauna.

- Take care when collecting wood, rocks or playing in snake environments.
- When travelling through the bush, wear boots and thick socks covered by very good pants like jeans.
- Carry a first aid kit and at least the two crepe bandages recommended for snakebite first aid.
- Observe and concentrate when walking along tracks.
- Watch out when stepping over logs, moving through dense grass tussocks etc.
- Avoid running in dense foliage or through tussock grasses. Keep children close to you.
- Be especially alert during the early parts of the day in spring and autumn particularly as snakes are sluggish and bask longer.
- Make ample room around snakes and move slowly when they are sighted.
- Never try to poke them, handle them or shoo them away.
- When walking in groups, rotate leaders to help keep a good lookout.
- Practise a drill for snakebite and other emergencies.
- Dogs should always be kept on a lead, when in areas where there are snakes.
- Teach children not to engage in risky behaviour such as sticking hands in holes or running through long grass.
- When camping, understand that a snake may have been there for several years before you came along for two days. In other words, respect the environment.
- Harassing, playing with or killing snakes in the bush is illegal, stupid and the easiest way to get bitten!
- During warmer months of the year, snakes (including venomous species) can be active at night. So a torch is essential.

Snake management plans

Snakes often enter buildings, mine sites, agricultural areas and farm sheds and offices. You should have a snake management plan which is tailored to suit what support you have from reptile catchers or staff within the workplace who may be trained to handle the snakes.

- Have designated staff on each shift or risk area, responsible for watching for snakes.
- A procedure for reporting sightings to management or an appointed supervisor.
- Appoint staff who can liase with catching personnel. They will need to ensure the snake is supervised from a safe distance and the area cleared to prevent confrontations.
- A list of help numbers and of snake catchers in manuals or on the wall.
- First aid compression bandages freely available in high-risk areas.
- An explanation of PIB – Pressure Immobilisation Bandaging – technique for staff.
- Check with your local hospital what antivenom they have (important for mines or other isolated ventures).
- Ensure a first aid appointed staff member has a snakebite procedure to follow.
- Ensure workers are not encouraged or permitted to handle or kill the snake. Enforce the plan to workers as procedure.

Workplace snake prevention

- Control and eradicate rodents from the region (if applicable).
- Ensure vegetation is properly managed and avoid high risk plants and excessive overgrowth.
- Identify any potential hiding or shelter sites and fill or remove.
- Encourage the stacking of miscellaneous workplace by-products, rubbish or debris away from areas of entry to the building or site.
- Manage the grass or lawn or similar areas to be as short as possible and vigorously maintained.
- Pay especial attention to any regions along walls, pathways, walkways and fence lines, use whipper-snippers to keep all grass down. Seal up any gaps or cracks in fence line.
- Use snake prevention barriers along wire fence if appropriate.
- Always call a catcher for advice on areas of concern or advice.

11 Dealing with snakebite

Despite overwhelming common belief, it will often take some provocation to make snakes strike and bite. However, some species, when surprised or cornered, have a strong, defensive behaviour either standing their ground or sometimes striking at the threat. Typically Eastern Brown Snakes and Coastal Taipans are animals of this nature. These two species are recognised as the most dangerous snakes to interact with, both by snake catchers and the public. Luckily for us these snakes are also very alert and most interactions never take place due to their nervous and vigilant nature. But remember, they are not aggressive and do not actively seek a confrontation. They have, however, established many defensive behaviours to deal with threats from larger animals such as humans.

Walking in the bush or around a property can sometimes bring an accidental encounter. Wearing boots and stout clothing such as jeans and thick socks will minimise the risk of snakebite.

Snakebite facts

- Stepping on a snake in the bush is viewed by the snake as an attack.
- Snakes will defend themselves when provoked.
- Some species are more defensive in nature.
- It often takes a very strong provocation to make snakes strike.
- A large proportion of bites can be avoided.
- Some snakes bite and do not inject venom.
- Snakes that are confused or cornered will rely on a threat display to see off the threat.
- Most snakes will bite as a last resort.
- Most domestic pets get bitten because they provoke or attack the snake.

Snakebite fallacies

- You can tell a harmless snake by its colour or shape.
- Snakes are more potent or aggressive after winter.
- A plague of snakes occurs.
- A saucer of milk will attract a snake.
- Pythons do not bite.
- Snakes cannot climb their own tail when handled.
- There are always two fang marks, puncture marks.
- If there are no fang marks, you have not been bitten.
- You need to have the snake at the hospital.
- You can die within an hour or faster.
- There is a shortage of antivenom.

The weather may also affect a snake's behaviour. For example, on hot days the snake may become overheated and is more easily provoked and more likely to become agitated. Also, if the snake has fed recently, its movement may be restricted and it is more likely to rely largely on a threat display for defence. A snake carrying eggs or embryos will find it more difficult to make a quick escape, and if it is in the process of sloughing (skin shedding), its eyesight may be temporarily impaired.

Snakebite can occur in a variety of ways and may not immediately be noticeable. Typically, a bite will present with fang scratches although sometimes no puncture is evident, or occasionally the classic two punctures may be evident. While pain is atypical, localised pain can occur, especially with bites from black snakes. Swelling may also be apparent. General symptoms may include headaches, nausea, vomiting, diarrhoea, abdominal pain and convulsions. In children, collapse and convulsions may be the first signs.

What is venom?

Venom is the fluid, which is secreted from the venom glands through the hollowed fangs of venomous snakes. This fluid is made up of proteins and enzymes that have several unique and vital functions.

An Inland Taipan from the remote inland plains of Queensland in classic threat display. Image: John Weigel.

Q What is a 'dry bite'?'

A Most venomous snakes have some control over when and how much venom they can inject. When surprised by being trodden on, a snake will bite but rarely inject venom – this is the classic 'dry bite'. However, if the snake is forewarned, a venomous bite is more likely.

Q Is the venom of a snake emerging from dormancy (winter slumber) more potent?

A This has never really been proven. Like saliva, venom can be restored quickly in the glands regardless what time of the year it is.

Q Are non-venomous snakes such as pythons venomous?

A In truth it has been revealed most snakes are actually mildly or very weakly venomous. Even some lizards have very primitive venom glands. While in extreme cases a person may have some very mild responses to these bites, it remains that they are considered harmless. There are some researchers who will examine these venoms very closely and over the next decade more will be known. Even people have toxins/enzymes in their saliva.

The aim of venom is to immobilise prey and the secondary components of the venom get to work, helping in digestion and possibly preservation of food. Venom is distinctive and variable between each genus, species and even within species populations.

Some species of venomous snakes have very small amounts of venom but its components are exceptionally powerfully neurotoxic e.g. Eastern Brown Snakes and Western Brown Snakes. Certain snake species have exceptionally large venom glands but less toxic neurotoxins; however, their venom contains very powerful myotoxins e.g. Mulga Snakes.

Generally speaking, the toxicity of the venom in each species reflects the prey types of that species. For example, mammal predators such as taipans have much stronger mammal-affecting neurotoxins than reptile-eating snakes such as copperheads and Mulga Snakes. Mammal-feeding snakes are more likely to have venom that is potentially harmful to humans.

Because of the variety of venom proteins and enzymes, different antivenoms are available for snakebite treatment. Snake venom strength and yield can be variable in a single species and from region to region. Other factors such as the snake's health, feeding frequency and its age can be relevant – older snakes have larger quantities and sometimes more toxic venom.

So what is the most venomous snake in Australia? This is a common question asked of snake catchers. If people are asking 'What snake has the most dangerous threat to a catcher personally when handling snakes?', it would be the Coastal Taipan or the Eastern Brown Snake. These two snakes have very nervous temperaments and the taipan has large fangs, powerful pro-coagulants and neurotoxins and large venom glands.

Laboratory tests have shown that the Inland Taipan has the most toxic venom in Australia.

Image: John Weigel.

Antivenom

Snakes are maintained in large colonies in order to be 'milked' at the Australian Reptile Park. The venom is is taken from snakes by pipette or 'mouthing' a beaker with a seal. The liquid venom is then processed and freeze dried.

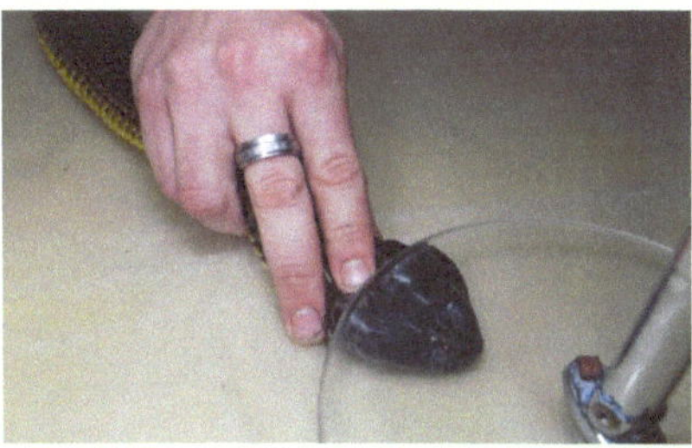

A herpetologist takes a Chappell Island Tiger Snake, restraining it safely.

The snake is encouraged to bite, in order to eject its venom.

The snake's fangs easily penetrate the vinyl diaphragm, and it ejects its venom.

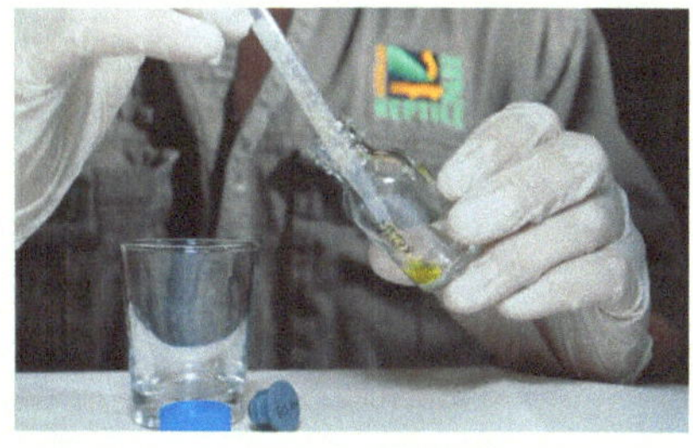

The herpetologist collects the venom and transfers it into a freeze-drying bottle.

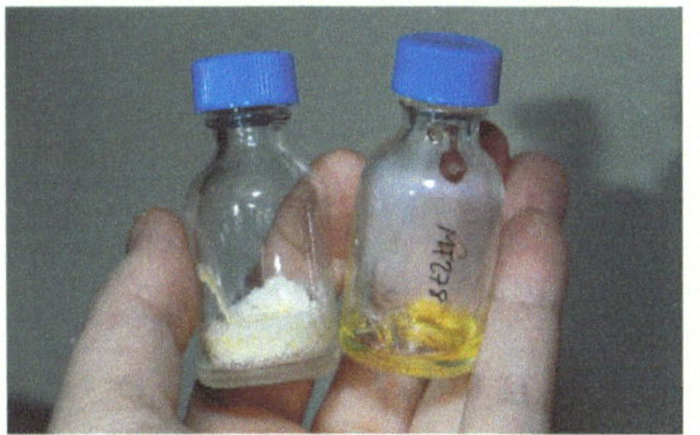

Freshly retrieved tiger snake venom (right) and a previously freeze-dried sample of approximately 100 mg (left).

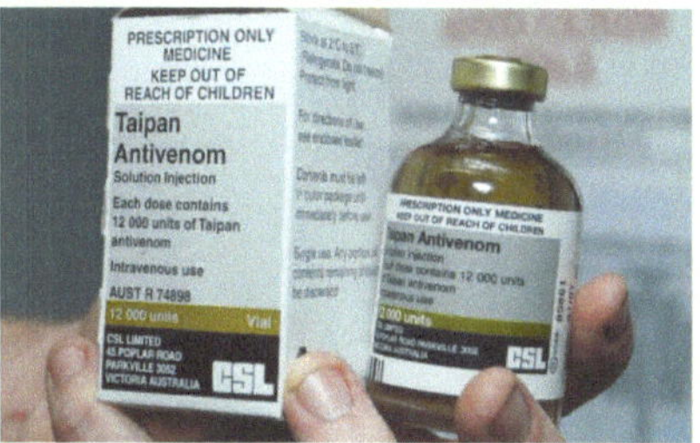

The Australian Reptile Park provides the raw snake venoms; CSL Ltd produces the life-saving antivenoms.

Image John Weigel

Snakebite and first aid

All bites should be treated as serious and first aid applied. Do not try to wait until clinical signs of snakebite occur before using the first aid.

Often a pin-prick pain is all that you may feel. Sometimes a bite from a snake will appear like scratches, which are made from their other teeth and not the fangs, so classic puncture marks are not definitive of venomous bites.

Australia leads the way in snakebite treatment with well trained medical staff, excellent hospital facilities and the availability of antivenom. We also have outstanding ambulance services, the Flying Doctor Service and a well-established mobile phone capability.

First aid, correctly applied, can delay the absorption of venom. The technique known as **PIB** – '**Pressure Immobilisation Bandaging**' – targets the lymphatic system, retarding the movement of the person's lymph fluid by the use of a firmly applied bandage. Using a splint in conjunction with the bandage further reduces any muscle-related movement of the lymph fluid. Applying the bandage does not prevent blood flow, which is an unwanted effect of a tourniquet.

Surveys of snakebite incidents in Australia have shown that the single most critical factor for a person's survival is the immediate application of **PIB**, without any delay. If a proper bandage is not available, any other piece of clothing – jeans, shirts, pantyhose – will make do.

Developed by the late Dr Struan Sutherland, **PIB** is a wonderful mix of ingenuity and simplicity. Usually this is sufficient treatment until the snakebite victim arrives at the nearest major hospital.

Q How tightly should I apply the crepe bandage?

A The bandage should be as tight as for a sprain. It remains more important that it's placed over the bite site as quickly as possible.

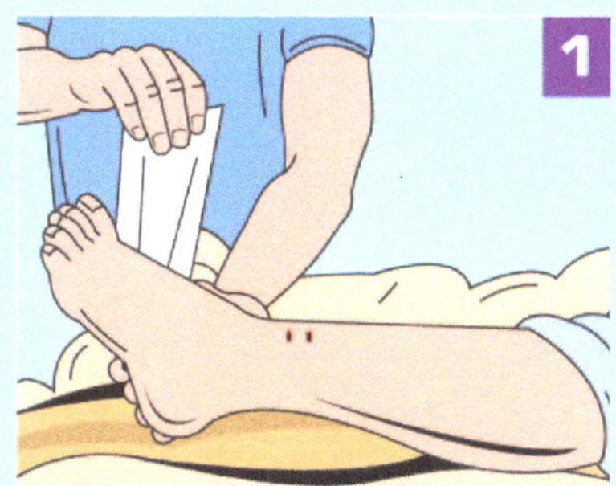

For a leg bite, start bandaging at the toes, but leave the tips of the toes unbandaged to allow the victim's circulation to be checked. It is not necessary to remove clothing.

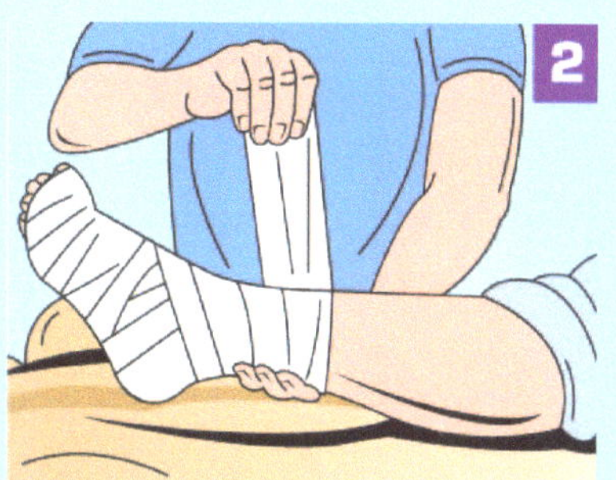

Bandage firmly as for a sprained ankle, but not so tight that circulation is prevented. Continue to bandage upward from the lower portion of the bitten limb.

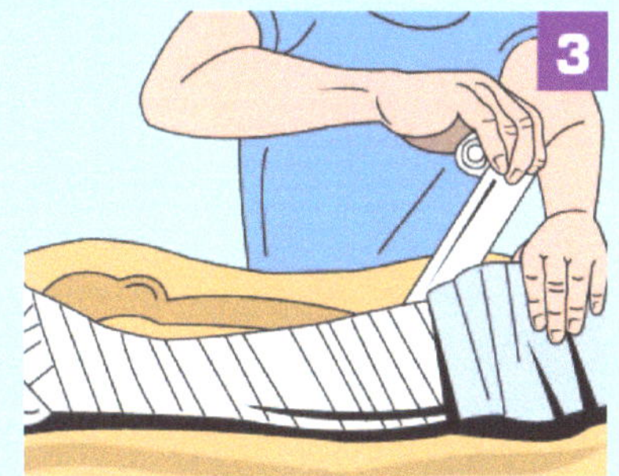

Apply the bandage as far up the limb as possible to compress the lymphatic vessels below the bite site and continue upward on the affected limb.

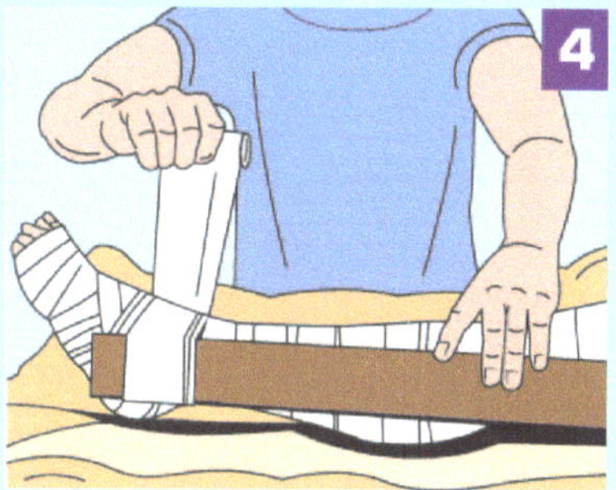

Use a splint to keep the bitten limb still. Secure the splint to the bandaged limb by using another bandage. If another bandage is not available, use clothing strips.

Bind the splint firmly to as much of the limb as possible to prevent muscle, limb and joint movement. This will restrict venom movement.

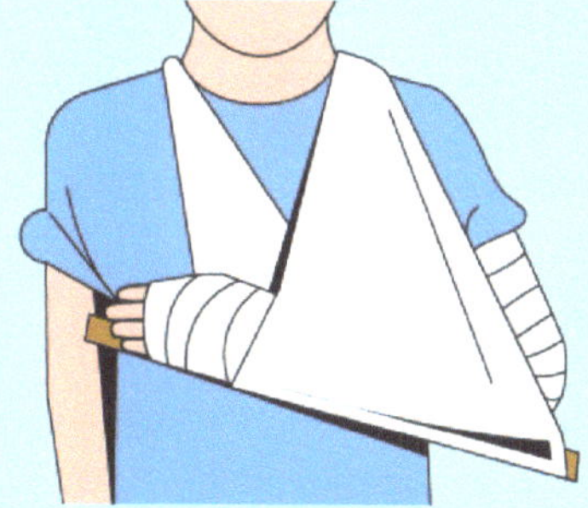

For a bite on the arm, apply a broad pressure bandage upward as far as possible leaving the tips of the fingers unbandaged, and bandaging the arm in a bent position.

In the event of snakebite

- Call 000 or 112, calling for an ambulance.
- Do not try to kill the snake.
- Apply first aid (PIB) even if the snake looks harmless.
- Remain with the patient, while you wait for help.
- Check the patient's blood flow in their toes or fingers.
- Commence CPR if the person becomes unresponsive.
- Do not apply a tourniquet.
- Do not cut the bite or attempt to suck the venom out.
- Do not use potassium permanganate crystals or solution near or on the bite wound.
- Do not wash or clean the bite.
- Do not leave the victim alone.
- Do not allow the victim to exercise or stress himself or herself.
- Do not apply ice to the wound.
- Do not take any aspirin.
- Do not let the victim drink any alcohol.

Use of the **PIB** technique will allow the snakebite victim time to be transported to a hospital where antivenom is available. The attending physician will usually take the bandage off only when the antivenom treatment is ready to be administered.

It is important for someone to remain with the snakebite victim to reassure them, offer them encouragement and humour them. If the victim collapses or becomes unresponsive, you should apply CPR till help arrives. It is important to remain calm, especially with children, as they can be more frightened by your emotions than the snake itself! Remember that the odds are high not only for survival but also for the snake to have not injected any venom.

Calling an ambulance

Call 000 to get an ambulance. Patients should never drive themselves or have someone drive them to hospital, unless absolutely unavoidable. Ambulance staff are well trained and experienced in many facets of medical care, they will know what hospital is best suited to treat you (as not all hospitals stock antivenom) and these people remain your best chance of medical care before arriving at the hospital. In some cases patients may be airlifted to major hospitals.

Snake identification

These days it is usually not necessary to identify the species of the offending snake. You should not attempt to kill it. However, if the snake is dead, it may help to have it safely stored, in the event that the attending doctor or a specialist requests to see it. A live snake should **never** be taken into a hospital. Nowadays we rely on several tests including a bite-site Venom Detection Kit (VDK), which can be used to determine the correct antivenom to treat the patient.

Q What if I intend to travel or work in a remote location within Australia?

A When travelling in areas where mobile coverage may be poor or unavailable, emergency calls to 000 or 112* may fail or mobile phones may be lost, damaged or have a flat battery. Ensure safety of all travelling by being prepared. Before going on trips into remote areas which may have poor mobile phone coverage, advise family members of destinations, intended routes to be followed, and timelines of arrivals and departures. Ensure you carry an alternative communications device, such as a satellite phone/subscription to an Australian satellite phone provider. Also seriously consider carrying a personal safety device, for example a Personal Locator Beacon (or EPIRB – Emergency Position-Indicating Radio Beacon). Aside from the unlikely chance of snakebite, it is more likely that other life-threatening emergencies could occur, such as bushfires, medical conditions or personal injury, flooding, car breakdowns, or becoming disorientated and/or lost.

*112 is the worldwide digital mobile (GSM) emergency number that connects to a country's emergency service automatically.

Snakebite in pets

Dogs and cats are vulnerable to the venom of some snake species, although some cats appear to be resistant to snakebite and seem to recover faster and are more able to survive.

Dogs get into trouble with snakes in backyards when they sense the snake by its movement or smell. There are two groups of dogs: one group are the biters or attackers that normally kill, play or retrieve wildlife. These breeds, including Jack Russells, Blue Heelers, German Shepherds and terriers, have a high risk of getting bitten. The other group, the barkers, normally keep barking at anything new or threatening. This group, including Labradors and poodles, have a better chance of surviving an encounter.

Signs of snakebite include dilated eyes, collapse or loss of consciousness, excessive salivation, diarrhoea and vomiting. The pet should be bandaged at the bite site using the PIB technique, and then taken immediately to your local veterinarian or 24-hr emergency pet centre. Antivenom and other tests are not cheap and associated costs may run into several thousands of dollars.

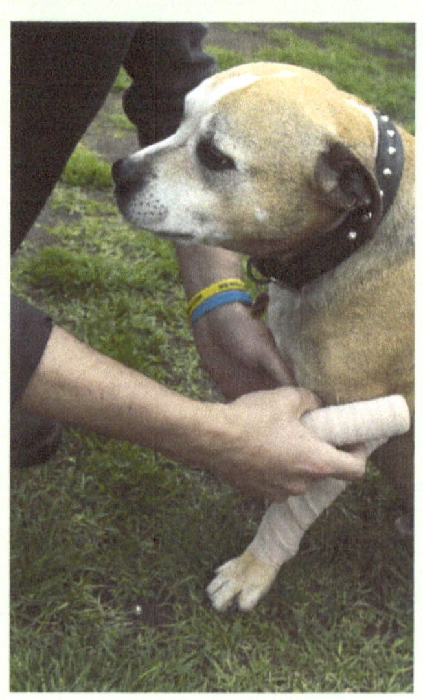

In some parts of northern Australia large predatory pythons may try to take a pet, for example a small dog, a cat or a large pet bird. Cats and dogs that are under predation by large pythons can be helped best by squirting or splashing a mixture of methylated spirits (or Dettol®, vodka or similar) with water into the mouth cavity of the reptile. This procedure will initially make the snake let go of the prey. The stinging of alcohol or even the effect of effervescent drinks, seems to work well. Don't interfere with the snake but leave it to uncoil itself. Often the pet can survive if it is still breathing. The snake may be confused and should not be handled.

Appendix

Legend: VC = Very common around premises, C = Common around properties, UC = uncommonly captured around residences, R = rarely seen or captured. Blank = not recorded in region.

Common 'nuisance' reptiles of New South Wales and Australian Capital Territory

	Sydney	South NSW	West NSW	North NSW	ACT
Blind Snakes (Typhlopidae)					
Ramphotyphlops nigrescens	UC	UC		UC	R
Ramphotyphlops spp.	R	R	R	R	
Pythons (Pythonidae)					
Spotted Python *Antaresia maculosa*				C	
Stimson's Python *Antaresia stimsoni*			C		
Morelia spilota spp.		C	C	C	
Diamond Python *Morelia spilota spilota*	VC	VC		VC	R
Colubrid Snakes (Colubridae)					
Brown Tree Snake *Boiga irregularis*	R	C		VC	
Common ('Green') Tree Snake *Dendrelaphis punctulatus*	VC	C		FC	
Keelback or Freshwater Snake *Tropidonophis mairii*				C	
Front Fanged Snakes (Elapidae)					
Common Death Adder *Acanthophis antarcticus*	R	R	R	UC	R
Lowland Copperhead *Austrelaps superbus*		UC			
Dwarf crowned Snake *Cacophis kreftti*		C			
Golden-crowned Snake *Cacophis squamulosus*	C			C	R
Yellow-faced Whip Snake *Demansia psammophis*	VC	UC	C	C	R
White-lipped Snake *Drysdalia coronoides*		C			
Red-naped Snake *Furina diadema*	C	C	C	C	R
Marsh Snake *Hemiaspis signata*	UC	C		C	
Stephens' Banded Snake *Hoplocephalus stephensii*				R	
Tiger Snake *Notechis scutatus*		UC		R	
Mulga Snake *Pseudechis australis*			C		
Spotted or Blue-bellied Black Snake *Pseudechis guttatus*				UC	
Red-bellied Black Snake *Pseudechis porphyriacus*	VC	VC		VC	R
Western Brown Snake *Pseudonaja nuchalis*			VC		
Eastern Brown Snake *Pseudonaja textilis*	VC	VC	VC	VC	VC
Eastern Small-eyed Snake *Rhinoplocephalus nigrescens*	UC	UC		UC	UC
Curl Snake *Suta suta*				UC	
Rough-scaled Snake *Tropidechis carinatus*				C	
Bandy Bandy *Vermicella annulata*	R	R	R	R	R
Introduced reptiles					
Asian House Gecko *Hemidactylus frenatus*				C	
Cane Toad *Bufo marinus*				C	

Common 'nuisance' snakes of Victoria

	Melbourne	West VIC	North VIC	East VIC
Pythons (Pythonidae)				
Diamond Python *Morelia spilota spilota*				UC Gippsland
Carpet Python *Morelia spilota* spp.			UC	
Front-fanged Snakes (Elapidae)				
Lowland Copperhead *Austrelaps superbus*	VC	C		C
White-lipped Snake *Drysdalia coronoides*	UC	C		C
Tiger Snake *Notechis scutatus*	VC	C	C	VC
Red-bellied Black Snake *Pseudechis porphyriacus*	R	R	VC	VC
Little Whip Snake *Parasuta flagellum*	UC		UC	
Eastern Brown Snake *Pseudonaja textilis*	VC	VC	VC	VC
Eastern Small-eyed Snake *Rhinoplocephalus nigrescens*	R		R	R

Common 'nuisance' snakes of South Australia

	Adelaide	West	North
Blind Snakes (Typhlopidae)			
Ramphotyphlops spp.		R	R
Pythons			
Stimson's Python *Antaresia stimsoni*		UC	UC
Carpet Python *Morelia spilota* spp.		UC	
Front-fanged Snakes (Elapidae)			
Common Death Adder *Acanthophis antarcticus*	R	UC	UC
Pygmy Copperhead *Austrelaps labialis*	R		
Yellow-faced Whip Snake *Demansia psammophis*		C	C
Red-naped Snake *Furina diadema*	VC	UC	UC
Tiger Snake *Notechis scutatus*	UC		
Krefft's Tiger Snake *Notechis ater ater*			R
Peninsula Tiger Snake *Notechis ater niger*		UC	
Mulga Snake *Pseudechis australis*		C	
Black-headed Snake *Parasuta nigreceps*		UC	UC
Red-bellied Black Snake *Pseudechis porphyriacus*	UC		
Dugite *Pseudonaja affinis*		R	
Western Brown Snake *Pseudonaja nuchalis*		VC	C
Peninsula Brown Snake *Pseudonaja inframacula*		C	
Eastern Brown Snake *Pseudonaja textilis*	VC	VC	C
Burrowing Snakes *Simoselaps* spp.		R	R
Curl Snake *Suta suta*		R	R
Bandy Bandy *Vermicella annulata*		R	R

Common 'nuisance' snakes of Queensland

	Brisbane	South QLD	West QLD	North QLD
Blind Snakes (Typhlopidae)				
Ramphotyphlops spp.	R	R	R	R
Ramphotyphlops nigrescens	R			
Ramphotyphlops polygrammicus	R			UC
Pythons (Pythonidae)				
Children's Python *Antaresia childreni*			C	
Spotted Python *Antaresia maculosa*				UC
Stimson's Python *Antaresia stimsoni*	C		C	
Black-headed Python *Aspidites melanocephalus*			C	UC
Water Python *Liasis fuscus*				R
Olive Python *Liasis olivaceus*			UC	
Scrub Python *Morelia kinghorni*				C
Carpet Python *Morelia spilota*	VC	VC		C
Colubrid Snakes (Colubridae)				
Brown Tree Snake *Boiga irregularis*	VC	VC		VC
Common ('Green') Tree Snake *Dendrelaphis punctulatus*				
Slaty-grey snake *Stegonotus cucullatus*				C
Keelback *Tropidonophis mairii*	VC	VC		VC
Front-fanged Snakes (Elapidae)				
Southern Death Adder *Acanthophis antarcticus*	C	R	C	R
Northern Death Adder *Acanthophis praelongus*		UC		
Northern Dwarf-crowned Snake *Cacophis churchilli*				C
White-crowned Snake *Cacophis harriettae*	C	C		
Yellow-faced Whip Snake *Demansia psammophis*	C	C	C	C
Lesser Black Whip Snake *Demansia vestigiata*		C	C	R
Red-naped Snake *Furina diadema*	UC	UC	C	R
Orange-naped Snake *Furina ornata*			C	
Marsh Snake *Hemiaspis signata*	C	C		UC
Stephens' Banded Snake *Hoplocephalus stephensii*	UC	UC		
Tiger Snake *Notechis scutatus*	R			
Coastal Taipan *Oxyuranus scutellatus*	R	R		R
Mulga Snake *Pseudechis australis*			C	R
Red-bellied Black Snake *Pseudechis porphyriacus*	C	C		C
Spotted Black Snake *Pseudechis guttatus*	R			
Northern Brown Snake (Gwardar) *Pseudonaja nuchalis*			VC	UC
Western Brown or Gwardar *Pseudonaja mengdeni*			VC	
Eastern Small-eyed Snake *Rhinoplocephalus nigrescens*	VC	VC		UC
Curl Snake *Suta suta*			C	R
Rough-scaled Snake *Tropidechis carinatus*	UC	C		UC
Bandy Bandy *Vermicella* spp.	R	R	R	R
Sea Snake	R			R

Common 'nuisance' reptiles of Queensland (contd)

	Brisbane	South QLD	West QLD	North QLD
Crocodiles				
Saltwater Crocodile *Crocodylus porosus*				UC
Freshwater Crocodile *Crocodylus johnstoni*				UC
Introduced reptiles				
Asian House Gecko *Hemidactylus frenatus*	VC	C	UC	VC
Cane Toad *Bufo marinus*	VC			UC

Common 'nuisance' snakes of Tasmania

	Hobart	Launceston	Islands
Front-fanged Snakes (Elapidae)			
Lowland Copperhead *Austrelaps superbus*	C	VC	VC
Eastern Tiger Snake *Notechis scutatus*	C	C	C
White-lipped Snake *Drysdalia coronoides*	C	C	C

Common 'nuisance' snakes of Northern Territory

Snakes	**Darwin**	**Central Aust**
Blind Snakes (Typhlopidae)		
Centralian Blind Snake *Ramphotyphlops centralis*		R
Robust Blind Snake *Ramphotyphlops ligatus*	R	
Pythons (Pythonidae)		
Children's Python *Antaresia childreni*	C	
Stimson's Python *Antaresia stimsoni*		VC
Black-headed Python *Aspidites melanocephalus*	C	
Water Python *Liasis fuscus*	VC	
Olive Python *Liasis olivaceus*	C	
Centralian Carpet Python *Morelia bredli*		C
Carpet Python *Morelia spilota variegata*	VC	
File Snakes (Acrochordidae)		
Arafura File Snake *Acrochordus arafurae*	UC	
Colubrid Snakes (Colubridae)		
Brown Tree Snake *Boiga irregularis*	VC	
Common Tree Snake *Dendrelaphis punctulata*	VC	
Slaty-grey Snake *Stegonotus cucullatus*	C	
Keelback *Tropidonophis mairii*	VC	
Front Fanged Snakes (Elapidae)		
Northern Death Adder *Acanthophis praelongus*	UC	
Desert Death Adder *Acanthophis pyrrhus*		R
Unbanded Shovel-nosed Snake *Brachyurophis incinctus*		UC
Yellow-faced Whip Snake *Demansia psammophis*		VC
Lesser Black Whip Snake *Demansia vestigiata*	C	
Orange-naped Snake *Furina ornata*	UC	UC
Mulga Snake *Pseudechis australis*	R	UC
Pygmy Mulga Snake *Pseudechis weigeli*	R	
Northern Brown Snake or Gwardar *Pseudonaja nuchalis*	VC	R
Western Brown or Gwardar *Pseudonaja mengdeni*		VC
Secretive Snake *Rhinoplocephalus pallidiceps*	R	
Little Spotted Snake *Suta punctata*		R
Curl Snake *Suta suta*		C
Northern Bandy Bandy *Vermicella intermedia*	R	
Bandy Bandy *Vermicella vermiformis*		R
Crocodiles		
Saltwater Crocodile *Crocodylus porosus*	UC	
Freshwater Crocodile *Crocodylus johnstoni*	UC	
Introduced Reptiles		
Asian House Gecko *Hemidactylus frenatus*	VC	
Flowerpot Blind Snake *Ramphotyphlops braminus*	R	
Cane Toad *Bufo marinus*	VC	

Common 'nuisance' snakes of Western Australia

	Perth	South WA	North WA
Blind Snakes (Typhlopidae)			
Southern Blind Snake *Ramphotyphlops australis*	R	R	R
Beaked Blind Snake *Ramphotyphlops waitii*	R		
Pythons (Pythonidae)			
Children's Python *Antaresia childreni*			VC
Stimson's Python *Antaresia stimsoni*	R	UC	VC
Black-headed Python *Aspidites melanocephalus*			C
Olive Python *Liasis olivaceus*			C
Carpet Python *Morelia spilota*	R	UC	R
Colubrid Snakes (Colubridae)			
Brown Tree Snake *Boiga irregularis*			VC
Front-fanged Snakes (Elapidae)			
Southern Death Adder *Acanthophis antarcticus*	R	R	
Desert Death Adder *Acanthophis pyrrhus*		R	UC
Pilbara Death Adder *Acanthophis wellsii*			UC
Yellow-faced Whip Snake *Demansia psammophis*	R	C	VC
Bardick *Echiopsis curta*	R	UC	
Western Crowned Snake *Elapognathus coronatus*	R	UC	
Orange-naped Snake *Furina ornata*			C
Black-naped Snake *Neelaps bimaculatus*	R		
Western Black-striped Snake *Neelaps calonotus*	R		
Western Tiger Snake *Notechis scutatus occidentalis*	R	C	
Gould's Hooded Snake *Parasuta gouldii*	UC	UC	
Mitchell's Short-tailed Snake *Parasuta nigriceps*	UC	UC	
Mulga Snake *Pseudechis australis*	R		C
Pygmy Mulga Snake *Pseudechis weigeli*			UC
Dugite *Pseudonaja affinis*	VC	VC	
Northern Brown Snake or Gwardar *Pseudonaja nuchalis*			C
Western Brown or Gwardar *Pseudonaja mengdeni*	R		VC
# Bandy Bandy *Vermicella annulata*			
# Northern Bandy Bandy *Vermicella multifasciata*			
Crocodiles			
Saltwater Crocodile *Crocodylus porosus*			R
Freshwater Crocodile *Crocodylus johnstoni*			R
Introduced species	**Perth**	**South**	**North**
Flowerpot Blind Snake *Ramphotyphlops braminus*	R		R
Cane Toad *Bufo marinus*			C

Glossary

adaptation An inherited (genetically controlled) characteristic of an organism that helps it to survive and reproduce in the environment it inhabits. These are often interpreted as evolutionary changes in response to selection pressures present in that environment.

antivenom Antivenoms are purified antibodies against venoms or venom components. Monovalent antivenom is a species-specific antivenom. Polyvalent antivenom targets all snake species.

carnivorous description of an animal, which primarily eats other animals.

caudal referring to the tail.

cloaca a body opening that serves both for excretion and for the reproductive organs.

clutch a group of eggs that is laid in the same place at the same time (or nearly the same time), and will hatch at the same time.

crepuscular active during the evening and early morning hours.

diurnal active during the day.

dormancy/dormant reptiles typically become inactive or dormant during cooler months of the year.

dorsal referring to features on the back or along the spine of the animal.

ectotherm an animal whose body temperature varies with the temperature of its surroundings (also called cold-blooded).

endotherm an animal that maintains its body temperature at a relatively constant level by physiological means regardless of the temperature of the environment (also called warm-blooded).

envenomation/envenoming the result of venom effects in the body.

genus in the classification of living things, a group of similar species. e.g. The black snake species all belong to the genus *Pseudechis*.

gravid carrying eggs or developing young.

gular relating to the throat of the animal.

habitat the kind of place where a plant or animal naturally lives.

herbivorous said of an animal that eats only plants.

herpetologist person who works or studies with reptiles.

insectivorous said of an animal which mostly eats insects.

keel a ridge down the centre of a scale. Very sharp keeling may make an animal appear quite rough.

lateral referring to the sides of the body. 'Laterally compressed' means flattened in such a way that the thing is high but not very wide.

live birth in reptiles, this is when the eggs hatch while still inside the female, and the young soon emerge alive. The young do not obtain nutrients from their mother while in the reproductive tract, as is the case with most mammals. A condition known as oviviviparous.

metamorphosis the developmental transition between larval and adult stages that can include extreme morphological transformations.

microhabitat where an animal lives in its niche.

nocturnal active primarily at night.

ophidiophobia the fear of snakes or snakebite.

oviparous reproduces by laying eggs.

ovoviviparous reproduces by eggs that remain in the mother's body until they are ready to hatch. When the young emerge, they are born live, with only a membrane to break out of.

snout-vent length a standard measurement, of body length. The measurement is from the tip of the nose (snout) to the anus (vent), and excludes the tail.

tail separation a defensive feature, found in many lizard species, where the tail vertebrae are easily broken, so that the tail will break off if it is grabbed by a predator. Same as 'caudal autonomy.'

toxin a substance, which has an adverse effect on physiology.

venom a chemical of biological origin (i.e. made by an animal) used by the animal for the purpose of attack or defence.

vent the cloaca of an animal; in reptiles this opening may also serve the reproductive organs. It is seen as a marker of where the body ends and the tail begins, which is hard to determine in some animals, such as snakes.

ventral referring to the underside of an animal, the 'tummy' side.

viviparous reproducing by giving birth to live young.

Useful contacts

EMERGENCY
Phone: 000
Out of range, phone: 112 (satellite phone only)
Poisons helpline: 131 126

Snakeline nationwide service for professional advice on snake problems, identification and help with finding snake catchers.
Phone: 1300 819 916
www. snakeline.com.au

ACT
Parks and Conservation, phone: 13 14 50
Southside, phone: (02) 6207 2127;
Northside, phone: (02) 6207 2113

NSW
National Parks and Wildlife
Phone: 1300 361 967

Wildlife and Information Rescue Service (WIRES),
Phone: 1300 094 737
www.wires.org.au/

Wildcare, phone: (02) 6299 1966
www.wildcare.com.au

VICTORIA
Department of Sustainability and Environment
www.dpi.vic.gov.au

Wildlife Victoria, phone: 1300 094 535

www.blacksnakeproductions.com.au

QUEENSLAND
Queensland Parks and Wildlife Service
Phone: (07) 3227 1111

Report crocodile sightings to the EPA Hotline
Phone: 1300 130 372

www.qm.qld.gov.au/features/snakes/index.asp

Far North Queensland Wildlife
Phone: (07) 4053 4467

Snake/Reptile catchers in the Brisbane/Gold Coast area
www.snakecatchers.com.au/
www.goldcoastsnakecatcher.com.au/
www.snakecatcher.com/

Australia Zoo Snake rescue
Phone: 1300 369 652

SOUTH AUSTRALIA
Fauna Rescue of S.A. Inc
P.O. Box 241
Modbury North
South Australia, 5092
Phone: (08) 8289 0896

Snake/Reptile catchers
Fauna Rescue
Phone: (08) 8289 0896

Adelaide Snake Catchers
Phone: 0413 665 483

www.livingwithwildlife.com.au
www.snake-away-services.websyte.com.au/

TASMANIA

Department of Primary Industry, Water and Environment, Nature Conservation Branch
Phone: (03) 6233 6556

Reptile Rescue Incorporated (24 hrs)
Phone: 0407 565 181

WESTERN AUSTRALIA

Conservation and Land Management (CALM), Wildlife Protection, Wildcare Helpline
Phone: (08) 9474 9055 (24 hrs)

Armadale Reptile Centre
304–308 South Western Hwy
Wungong WA 6112
Phone: (08) 9399 6927

Snake/Reptile catchers
members.iinet.net.au/~bush/index.html

NORTHERN TERRITORY

Darwin and Darwin Rural Snake Callout, phone: phone: 1800 453 210

Ark Animal Hospital, phone: (08) 8932 9738 – Yarrawonga, cnr of Callanan Rd and Georgina Crescent
Ark Animal Hospital, phone: (08) 8988 3340 – Humpty Doo, 12 Verker Street

Snake/Reptile catchers
Darwin, Palmerston and rural areas
Phone: 1800 453 210
Katherine
Phone: 0407 934 252
Alice Springs
Phone: 0407 983 276

Report a crocodile sighting
Darwin, phone: 0419 822 859 or (08) 8999 4691
Katherine, phone: 0407 958 405 or (08) 8973 8888

MEDICAL/PROFESSIONAL HELP

Australian Venom Research Unit
Phone: 1300 760 451
www.avru.org

Australian Venom Research Unit
Department of Pharmacology
University of Melbourne
Parkville, VIC, 3010. Australia
Phone: (03) 8344 7753

Venom Supplies
Peter Mirtshin
PO Box 547
Tanunda
South Australia 5352
Phone: (08) 8563 0001
www.venomsupplies.com

CSL Limited
Registered Head Office
45 Poplar Rd
Parkville
Victoria 3052
Australia
Phone: (03) 9389 1911
Fax: (03) 9389 1434
http://www.csl.com.au

CSL Bioplasma Immunohaematology
Phone: (03) 9389 1911
Email: antivenom@csl.com.au

OTHER USEFUL WEBSITES

www.snakebiteinitiative.org
www.pestat.com.au
toadtrap.com.au
www.canetoadsinoz.com
www.canetoads.com.au/
www.frogwatch.org.au
www.frogsaustralia.net.au/frogs

References

Broad AJ, Sutherland SK and Coulter AR (1979) The lethality in mice of dangerous Australian and other snake venom. *Toxicon* **17**, 661–664.

Bradley C and Harrison J (2008) 'Hospital separations due to injury and poisoning, Australia 2004–05'. Injury Research and Statistics Series Number 47. Australian Institute of Health and Welfare, Canberra.

Bush B, Maryan B, Browne-Cooper R and Robinson D (2010) *Field Guide to Reptiles of the Perth Region*. Western Australian Museum, Perth.

Cann J (1986) *Snakes Alive. Snake Experts and Antidote Sellers of Australia*. Kangaroo Press, Sydney.

Clayton M, Wombey JC, Mason IJ, Chesser RT and Wells A (2006) *CSIRO List of Australian Vertebrates: A Reference with Conservation Status*. CSIRO Publishing, Melbourne.

Cogger HG (2000) *Reptiles & Amphibians of Australia*. Reed New Holland, Sydney.

Covacevich J, Davie P and Pearn J (Eds) (1987) *Toxic Plants and Animals: A Guide for Australia*. Queensland Museum, Brisbane.

Currie BJ (2006) Treatment of snakebite in Australia: the current evidence base and questions requiring collaborative multicentre prospective studies. *Toxicon* **48**(7), 941–956.

Ehmann H (1992) Reptiles. In: *Encyclopaedia of Australian Animals*. (Ed. R Strahan) Vol 3. Australian Museum and Angus & Robertson, Sydney.

Fearn S (1993) The Tiger Snake *Notechis scutatus* (Serpentes: Elapidae) in Tasmania. *Herpetofauna* **23**(2), 17–29.

Fearn S (1994) Some observations on the ecology of the Copperhead *Austrelaps superbus* (Serpentes Elapidae) in Tasmania. *Herpetofauna* **24**(2), 1–10.

Fearn S, Robinson B, Sambono J and Shine R (2001) Pythons in the pergola: the ecology of 'nuisance' carpet pythons (*Morelia spilota*) from suburban habitats in south-eastern Queensland. *Wildlife Research* **28**, 573–579.

Fry BG, Winkel DK, Wickramaratna JC, Hodgson W and Wuster W (2003) Effectiveness of snake antivenom: species and regional venom variation and its clinical impact. *Journal of Toxicology* **22**(1), 23–24.

Gow GF (1989) *Graeme Gow's Complete Guide to Australian Snakes*. Angus & Roberston, Sydney.

Grifiths K (2005) *Frogs and Reptiles of the Sydney Region*. Botanic Garden Trust, Sydney.

Mirtschin P and Davies R (1992) *Snakes of Australia: Dangerous and Harmless*. Hill of Content, Melbourne.

Morrison JJ, Pearn JH, Covacevich J and Nixon J (1983) Can Australians identify snakes? *Medical Journal of Australia* **2**, 66–70.

Shine R (1977) Habitats, diet and sympatry in snakes: a study from Australia. *Canadian Journal of Herpetology* **55**, 1118–1128.

Shine R (1987a) Ecological comparisons of island and mainland populations of Australian tiger snakes (*Notechis Elapidae*). *Herpetologica* **43**(2), 233–240.

Shine R (1987b) Ecological ramifications of prey size: food habits and reproductive biology of Australian copperhead snakes (*Austrelaps, Elapidae*). *Journal of Herpetology* **21**, 21–28.

Shine R (1989) Constraints, allometry and adaptation: food habits and reproductive biology of Australian brown snakes *(Pseudonaja, Elapidae*). *Herpetologica* **45**, 195–207.

Shine R (1991) *Snakes: A Natural History*. Reed Books, Sydney.

Shine R and Koenig J (2001) Snakes in the garden: an analysis of reptiles 'rescued' by community-based wildlife carers. *Biological Conservation* **102**, 271–283.

Sprivulus P, Jelinek GA and Marshall L (1996) Efficacy and potency of antivenoms in neutralising the procoagulant effects of Australian snake venoms in dog and human plasma. *Anaesthesia and Intensive Care* **24**, 379–381.

Sutherland SK (1983) *Australian Animal Toxins: The Creatures, Their Toxins and Care of the Poisoned Patient*. Oxford University Press, Melbourne.

Sutherland SK (1992a) Deaths from snake bite in Australia, 1981–1991. *Medical Journal of Australia* **157**(11–12), 740–746.

Sutherland SK (1992b) Antivenom use in Australia: premedication, adverse reactions and the use of venom detection kits. *Medical Journal of Australia* **157**(11–12), 734–739.

Sutherland SK (1994) *Venomous Creatures of Australia*. Oxford University Press, Melbourne.

Sutherland SK, Coulter AR and Harris RD (1979) The rationalization of first aid measures for elapid snake bite. *Lancet* **1**, 183–186.

Sutherland SK and King K (1991) *Management of Snake Bite in Australia*. Royal Flying Doctor Service of Australia Monograph Series No.1.

Sutherland SK and Leonard RL (1995) Snake bite deaths in Australia 1992–1994 and a management update. *Medical Journal of Australia* **163**, 616–618.

Swan M and Watharow S (2005) *Snakes, Lizards and Frogs of the Victorian Mallee*. CSIRO Publishing, Melbourne.

Swaroop S and Grab B (1954) Snake bite mortality in the world. *Bulletin of the World Health Organisation* **10**, 35–76.

Tibballs J (1992) Diagnosis and treatment of confirmed and suspected snake bite: implications from an analysis of 46 paediatric cases. *Medical Journal of Australia* **156**, 270–274.

Watharow S (1997) Ecology of Eastern Tiger Snake *Notechis scutatus* and Lowland Copperhead *Austrelaps superbus* within metropolitan Melbourne. *'Monitor': Journal of Victorian Herpetological Society* **8**(3), 145–151.

Watharow S (1998) Dietary and parasite observations of roadkilled reptiles from north-western Victoria. *'Monitor': Journal of Victorian Herpetological Society* **10**(1), 51–60.

Watharow S (1999a) Oophagy in Lowland Copperhead *Austrelaps superbus* (*Elapidae*) in the Melbourne metropolitan area. *Herpetofauna* **29**(1), 19–20.

Watharow S (1999b) Aspects of mortality and natural history in elapid snakes from Melbourne, Australia. *'Monitor': Journal of Victorian Herpetological Society* **10**(2/3), 46–56.

Watharow S (1999c) Snake control and the benefits for translocated Snakes. *'Monitor': Journal of Victorian Herpetological Society* **10**(2/3), 59–64.

Watharow S (2000) Egg incubation methods and juvenile dispersal of Eastern Brown Snakes (*Pseudonaja textilis*). *'Monitor': Journal of Victorian Herpetological Society* **11**(1), 16–17.

Watharow S (2001a) A field trip to Flinders Island, Tasmania with a dash of Mt Chappell please. *'Monitor': Journal of Victorian Herpetological Society* **11**(2), 9–16.

Watharow S (2001b) Prevalence of the plerocercoid of *Spirometra erinacei* (Cestoda) in three species of elapid snakes in the Melbourne region. *Herpetofauna* **31**(1), 28–33.

Watharow S and Reid A (2002) The introduced snake mite *Ophinyssus natricis* on wild populations of eastern blue tongue lizards (*Tiliqua scincoides*). *Herpetofauna* **32**(1), 26–29.

Watharow S (2002) Diets of three large elapid snakes from the Melbourne metropolitan region. *Herpetofauna* **32**(1), 30–34.

Wilson S and Swan G (2005) *A Complete Guide to Reptiles of Australia*. New Holland Publishers, Sydney.

Webb G and Manolis C (2009) *Crocodiles of Australia*. New Holland, Sydney.

White J (1987) Elapid snakes: venom toxicities and actions. In: *Toxic Plants and Animals: A Guide for Australia*. (Eds J Covacevich, P Davie and J Pearn) pp. 369–389. Queensland Museum, Brisbane.

White J (1998) Envenoming and antivenom use in Australia. *Toxicon* **36**(11), 1483–1492.

White J (2000) Why do people still die from brown snake bites? *Emergency Medicine* **12**(3), 204–206.

Index

www.ingramcontent.com/pod-product-compliance
Lightning Source LLC
LaVergne TN
LVHW052251100826
845147LV00001B/14

* 9 7 8 0 6 4 3 0 9 7 2 1 6 *